Software Recipes
Proven Tools

by D. James Benton

Copyright © 2022 by D. James Benton, all rights reserved.

Preface

This text describes a collection of compact, efficient, and effective software scripts. These code tools can be deployed in several forms, including C, VBA, and Python, to perform a variety of common computing tasks. This text differs from the classic text, *Numerical Recipes: The Art of Scientific Computing* by Press, Teukolsky, Vetterling, and Flannery, in both form and detail. While the title of this classic text (Numerical Recipes) might sound like a collection of small codes, it is actually a complete volume on numerical methods. I have already written several texts on that larger and more detailed subject, which will not be repeated here. To utilize the material in this text, locate the chapter describing the desired task, copy the code therein, and paste it into your application or spreadsheet.

All of the examples contained in this book,
(as well as a lot of free programs) are available at...
https://www.dudleybenton.altervista.org/software/index.html

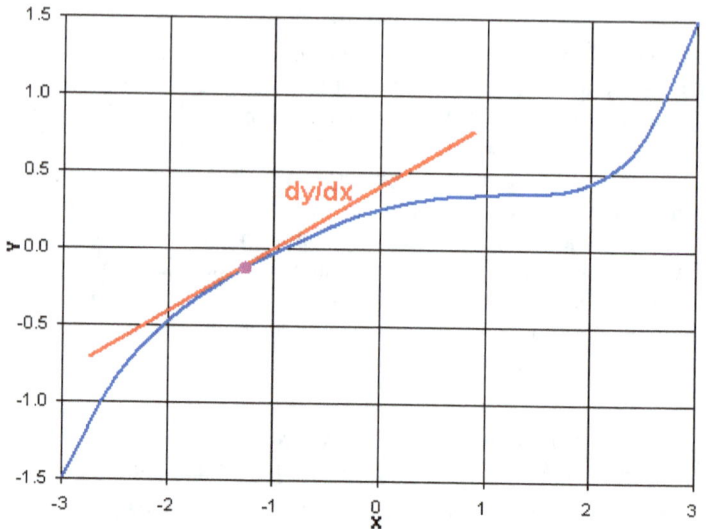

Figure 1. Finding the Slope of a Function at a Point

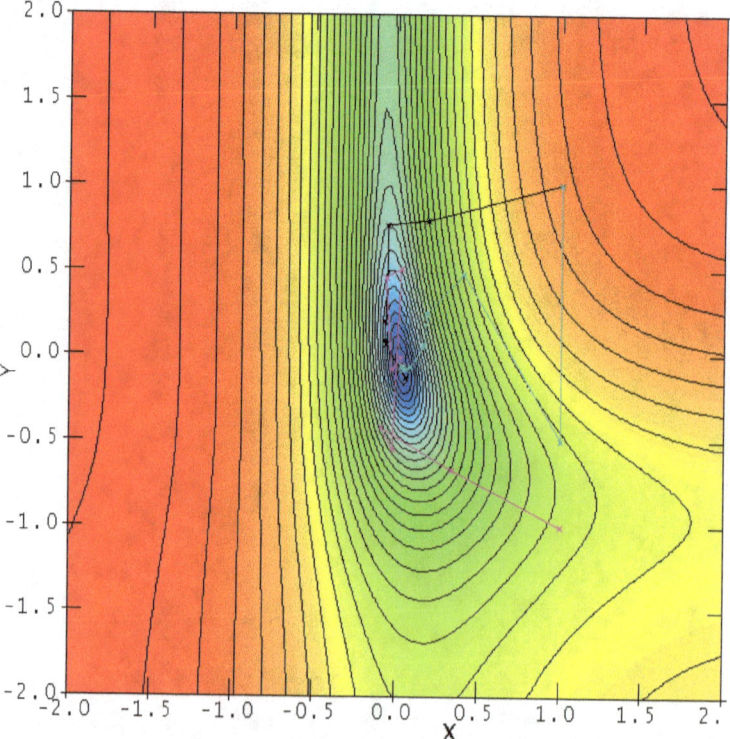

Figure 2. Finding the Minimum of a Function of Two Variables

Table of Contents

	page
Preface	i
Chapter 1. Interpolation/Table Look-Up	1
Chapter 2. Lagrange Interpolation	9
Chapter 3. Cubic Splines	11
Chapter 4. Bisection Search	15
Chapter 5. Secant Method	17
Chapter 6. Using the Excel™ Solver	19
Chapter 7. Using Excel's LINEST	21
Chapter 8. Using qsort()	31
Chapter 9. Insertion Sort	35
Chapter 10. Test for Inside Polygon	41
Chapter 11. Inverse Distance Interpolation	45
Chapter 12. Kriging	49
Chapter 13. Simultaneous Linear Equations	51
Chapter 14. Linear Equations with Linear Constraints	55
Chapter 15. Nonlinear Optimization in One Dimension	57
Chapter 16. Nonlinear Optimization in Multiple Dimensions	59
Chapter 17. Fast Fourier Transform and Beyond	63
Chapter 18. Random Numbers	77
Chapter 19. Predicting a Trend or Storm	81
Appendix A. Sample Excel™ Add-In	91
Appendix B. Normal Distribution Functions	93
Appendix C. Digitizing Curves	97
Appendix D. Curve-Fitting	99
Appendix E. Graphing Data	101
Appendix F. Editing Polygons	105

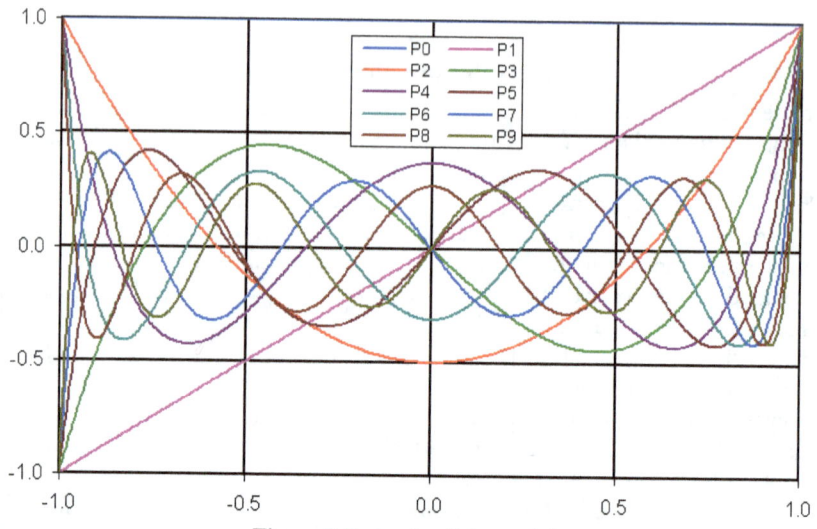

Figure 3. Legendre Polynomials

	A	B	C	D	E	F	G	H	I	J	K	L	M	N	O	P
1			Chebyshev polynomials of the 1st kind							orthogonality test						
2	x	w	T0	T1	T2	T3	T4	T5			T0	T1	T2	T3	T4	T5
3	-1.00	4.11	1.000	-1.000	1.000	-1.000	1.000	-1.000	T0	62	0	-1	0	0	0
4	-0.95	3.20	1.000	-0.950	0.805	-0.580	0.296	0.017	T1	0	31	0	0	0	1
5	-0.90	2.29	1.000	-0.900	0.620	-0.216	-0.231	0.632	T2	-1	0	31	0	0	0
6	-0.85	1.90	1.000	-0.850	0.445	0.094	-0.604	0.933	T3	0	0	0	32	0	1
7	-0.80	1.67	1.000	-0.800	0.280	0.352	-0.843	0.997	T4	0	0	0	0	32	0
8	-0.75	1.51	1.000	-0.750	0.125	0.563	-0.969	0.891	T5	0	1	0	1	0	33

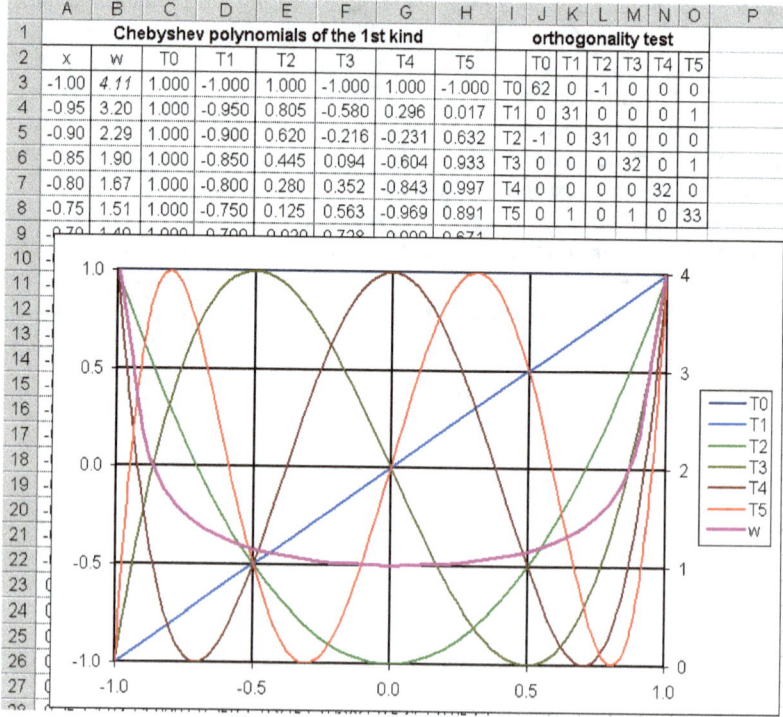

Figure 4. Chebyshev Polynomials

Chapter 1. Interpolation/Table Look-Up

Perhaps the most basic and frequent task is interpolation. This often is simply a table look-up, which is piecewise continuous. We will consider higher order infinitely continuous interpolation in Chapter 2. We first consider a typical data set.

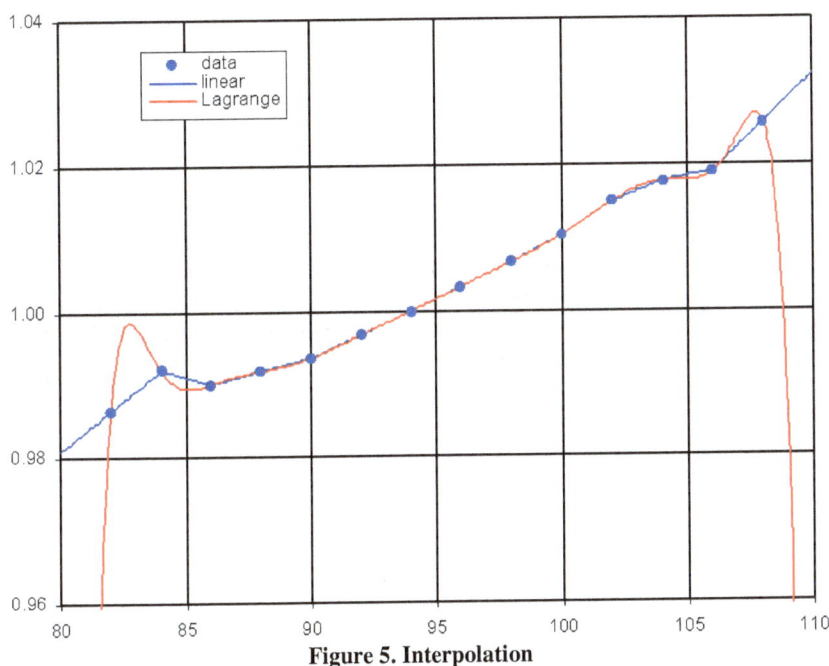

Figure 5. Interpolation

The core of the VBA macro might be:

```
Function LinearInterpolation1(Xp As Range, Yp As Range,
    X As Double) As Double
  Dim i As Integer
  For i = 2 To Xp.Count
    If (X >= Xp(i - 1) And X <= Xp(i)) Then
      LinearInterpolation1 = Yp(i - 1) + _
      (Yp(i) - Yp(i - 1)) * (X - Xp(i - 1)) _
      / (Xp(i) - Xp(i - 1))
      Exit Function
    End If
  Next i
End Function
```

There are 2 problems with this algorithm: 1) it only works if Xp is always increasing; 2) it doesn't work if X is outside the range of the list (less than the lowest or more than the highest). We can easily fix the first problem with a simple change:

```
        If ((X - Xp(j - 1)) * (X - Xp(j)) <= 0) Then
```
We could fix the second problem by adding two tests:
```
        If (X < Xp(1)) Then
            ...
        If (X > Xp(Xp.Count)) Then
            ...
```

But these two if()then statements only work if Xp is always increasing. If we want to handle the case where Xp is always decreasing (some user will do it), that would require four compound if()then statements. We could combine these into one compound statement using the Abs() function:

If (Abs(X - Xp(1)) < Abs(X - Xp(Xp.Count))) Then

I once had a spreadsheet that would sporadically mess up. I eventually tracked the problem down to a simple linear interpolation macro. Everything looked OK but it didn't always work. Why? In Excel™ we are not only working with floating-point numbers but also *interpreted* code. The if()then statements didn't always work as expected due to roundoff. I implemented the following simple fix:

```
Function LinearInterpolation2(Xp As Range, Yp As Range,
  X As Double) As Double
    Dim i As Integer, j As Integer
    i = -1
    For j = 2 To Xp.Count
        If ((X - Xp(j - 1)) * (X - Xp(j)) <= 0) Then
            i = j
            Exit For
        End If
    Next j
    If (i < 1) Then
        If (Abs(X - Xp(1)) < Abs(X - Xp(Xp.Count))) Then
            i = 2
        Else
            i = Xp.Count
        End If
    End If
    LinearInterpolation2 = Yp(i - 1) + (Yp(i) - Yp(i - 1))
   * (X - Xp(i - 1)) / (Xp(i) - Xp(i - 1))
End Function
```

By first setting i to −1 if for any reason the loop doesn't find a pair that satisfies the test, the procedure reverts to the Abs() test, providing a reasonable result. The data, graphic, and code may be found in the online archive accompanying this text in folder \examples and spreadsheet interpolation.xls.

Very Large Tables

Before we leave this topic, we consider very large tables (hundreds or even thousands of entries). In this case, the loop above can be quite slow. The case in point arose from temperature data provided by the NWS once every 4 hours. The calculations were required hourly so that interpolation was necessary to fill in the gaps. The data consist of 2190 values (365*8) requiring 8760 interpolations (365*24). The previous algorithm (LinearInterpolation2) requires several minutes to process, while the following algorithm (LinearInterpolation3) takes only a few seconds. The difference is a bisection search, which we will cover in Chapter 5. The data, graphic, and code may be found in the examples folder in spreadsheet temperatures.xls. The data is shown in the figure below:

	A	B	C	D
1	Interpoating a Large Table			
2	date:time	°F	date:time	°F
3	1/1/2021 2:00	9	1/1/2021 0:00	10.0
4	1/1/2021 6:00	7	1/1/2021 1:00	9.5
5	1/1/2021 10:00	6	1/1/2021 2:00	9.0
6	1/1/2021 14:00	17	1/1/2021 3:00	8.5
7	1/1/2021 18:00	26	1/1/2021 4:00	8.0
8	1/1/2021 22:00	19	1/1/2021 5:00	7.5
9	1/2/2021 2:00	12	1/1/2021 6:00	7.0
10	1/2/2021 6:00	10	1/1/2021 7:00	6.8
11	1/2/2021 10:00	10	1/1/2021 8:00	6.5
12	1/2/2021 14:00	23	1/1/2021 9:00	6.3
13	1/2/2021 18:00	30	1/1/2021 10:00	6.0
14	1/2/2021 22:00	29	1/1/2021 11:00	8.7
15	1/3/2021 2:00	28	1/1/2021 12:00	11.5
16	1/3/2021 6:00	25	1/1/2021 13:00	14.2
17	1/3/2021 10:00	25	1/1/2021 14:00	17.0
18	1/3/2021 14:00	27	1/1/2021 15:00	19.2
19	1/3/2021 18:00	31	1/1/2021 16:00	21.5
20	1/3/2021 22:00	31	1/1/2021 17:00	23.7
21	1/4/2021 2:00	31	1/1/2021 18:00	26.0
22	1/4/2021 6:00	31	1/1/2021 19:00	24.3
23	1/4/2021 10:00	31	1/1/2021 20:00	22.5
24	1/4/2021 14:00	33	1/1/2021 21:00	20.8
25	1/4/2021 18:00	35	1/1/2021 22:00	19.0
26	1/4/2021 22:00	34	1/1/2021 23:00	17.3

Figure 6. Temperature Data and Interpolation

The VBA code is listed below:

```
Function LinearInterpolation3(Xp As Range, Yp As Range, ByVal X As Double) As Double
   Dim i As Long, i1 As Long, i2 As Long, j As Long
   If (X <= Xp(1)) Then
      i = 1
   ElseIf (X >= Xp(Xp.Count)) Then
      i = Xp.Count - 1
   Else
      i1 = 1
      i2 = Xp.Count
      For j = 1 To 32
```

```
      i = (i1 + i2) \ 2
      If (i = i1) Then
         Exit For
      ElseIf (X > Xp(i + 1)) Then
         i1 = i
      ElseIf (X < Xp(i)) Then
         i2 = i
      Else
         Exit For
      End If
   Next j
   End If
   LinearInterpolation3 = Yp(i) + (Yp(i + 1) - Yp(i)) *
   (X - Xp(i)) / (Xp(i + 1) - Xp(i))
   End Function
```

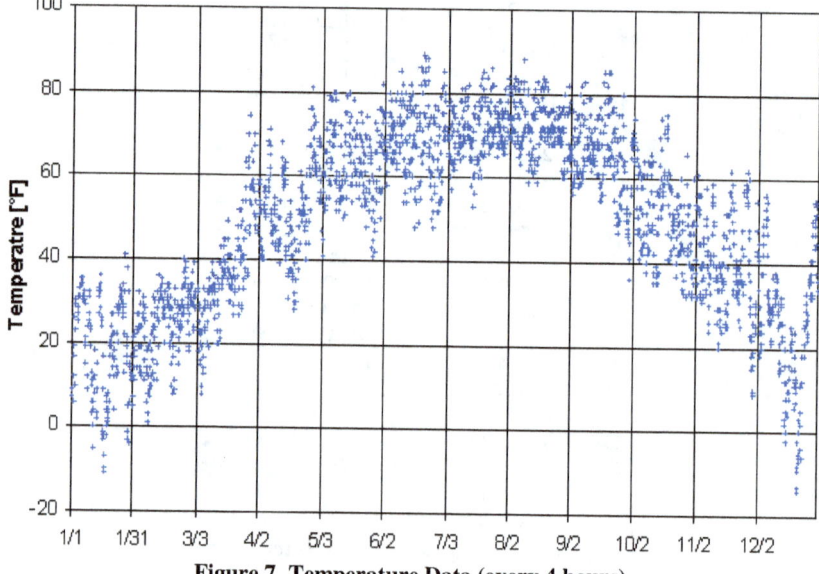

Figure 7. Temperature Data (every 4 hours)

This is a standard table look-up with linear interpolation plus a bisection search. 'The bisection search makes a HUGE difference when you have big tables and adds very little overhead when you have small tables. The table must be in ascending order. Note the backslash on the line above (i=(i1+i2)\2). This is actually an integer divide. Excel presumes all operations are type "variant" (actually, floating-point), which is clearly not true when all of the operators are integers. If you use a forward slash (/, the usual symbol for divide) this algorithm will not work.

Bi-Variate Interpolation

Interpolation in two dimensions is a fairly common task. This can implemented easily in C or VBA inside an Excel spreadsheet. An example might be finding the elevation along a path or road from a table representing a topographic map. The example use here is Western Cape Code, shown below:

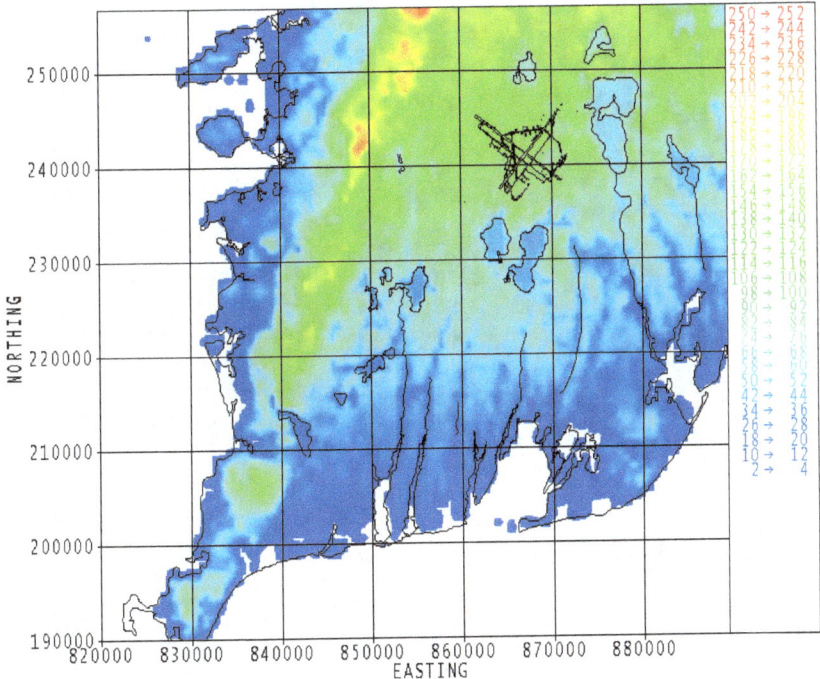

Figure 8. Western Cape Cod Elevations

The horizontal axis shows Universal Transverse Mercator Easting and the vertical axis shows Northing. These are common map coordinates. The colors indicate elevation in meters above mean sea level. The color scale is shown on the right.

The simplest approach to this problem is to create table in Excel having the X values across the top, which need not necessarily be evenly spaced, and the Y values in a column on the left. Fill the rectangle of cells within these edges with the Z values, as illustrated below:

	A	B	C	D	E	F	G	H	I
1		Surface Elevation of Western Cape Cod in Meters above Mean Sea Level							
2		Universal Transverse Mercator Easting in meters								Ur
3	northing	826349	827099	827849	828599	829349	830099	830849	831599
4	188575	0	0	0	0	0	0	0.2	0.1
5	189325	0	0	0.1	0	0	0.1	15.9	4.2
6	190075	0	0.2	1.2	0.1	26.4	4.5	16.5	1.6
7	190825	0	1.3	10	4.5	56.7	44.9	25.9	19.7
8	191575	0	2.4	2.9	3.9	36.3	61.6	25.4	49.7
9	192325	1.2	1.2	43.3	47.9	83.4	74.5	21.5	47.7
10	193075	14.9	0.9	20.7	51.5	105.3	68.7	56.9	26.4
11	193825	1.3	2.6	30	57.2	91.8	85.8	31.3	31.7
12	194575	0.1	13	41.8	79.4	91.2	87.3	65.6	36.7
13	195325	0	1	34.2	73.9	88.8	79.5	71.7	72.5
14	196075	0	0.3	63.5	51.4	79.7	47.1	54.9	69.7
15	196825	0	0	18.4	4.1	5.3	25.6	24.4	68
16	197575	0	0	2.4	0.7	0	0	0.2	43.2
17	198325	0	0	0	0	0	0	0.1	1.3
18	199075	0	0	0	0	0	0.5	15.2	0
19	199825	0	0	0	0	0	0	9.2	22
20	200575	0	0	0	0	0	0	11.2	30.6
21	201325	0	0	0	0	0	0	0	20.1
22	202075	0	0	0	0	0	0	0	4.5
23	202825	0	0	0	0	0	0	0	7
24	203575	0	0	0	0	0	0	0	6.2
25	204325	0	0	0	0	0	0	0.4	6.9
26	205075	0	0	0	0	0	0	0	2.2
27	205825	0	0	0	0	0	0	0	1.6

Figure 9. Typical 2D Table Setup in Excel

The interpolation is linear in X and Y. We first find the index of the appropriate pair of columns along the top (X) and then along the side (Y), then perform the double linear interpolation. The VBA code is listed below:

```
Function Interpolate2D(Z As Range, X, Y) As Variant
    Dim i As Integer, j As Integer, X1 As Double,
    X2 As Double, Y1 As Double, Y2 As Double
    Dim Z11 As Double, Z12 As Double, Z21 As Double,
    Z22 As Double, Za As Double, Zb As Double
    j = 2
    While (j < Z.Columns.Count - 1 And Z(1, j+1) < X)
        j = j + 1
    Wend
    i = 2
```

```
    While (i < Z.Rows.Count - 1 And Z(i+1, 1) < Y)
        i = i + 1
    Wend
    X1 = Z(1, j)
    X2 = Z(1, j + 1)
    Y1 = Z(i, 1)
    Y2 = Z(i + 1, 1)
    Z11 = Z(i, j)
    Z12 = Z(i, j + 1)
    Z21 = Z(i + 1, j)
    Z22 = Z(i + 1, j + 1)
    Za = Z11 + (Z12 - Z11) * (X - X1) / (X2 - X1)
    Zb = Z21 + (Z22 - Z21) * (X - X1) / (X2 - X1)
    Interpolate2D = Za + (Zb - Za) * (Y - Y1) / (Y2 - Y1)
End Function
```

The path of interest and interpolated elevation looks like this:

CH	CI	CJ
road path		
easting	northing	elevation
838298	196279	0.0
841010	197946	0.0
843734	199591	8.5
846468	201220	4.1
849196	202859	5.2
851766	204724	4.5
853146	207423	20.9
851613	210143	27.5
849843	212685	37.1
851140	215150	42.4

Figure 10. Interpolation along a Path

The function is called thus:

`=Interpolate2D($A$3:$CG$94,CH3,CI3)`

Implementation in C is almost identical to this, except for the initial index because C arrays begin at zero. The data and code can be found in interp2d.xls

Chapter 2. Lagrange Interpolation

When a series of connected straight line segments are not adequate, the next most attractive option is Lagrange interpolation; that is, a polynomial that fits exactly at three or more points. This works quite well but can exhibit wild excursions at high order (many points), in which case we employ a cubic spline, which will be described in Chapter 3. Lagrange interpolation is a powerful tool and quite simple to implement. It is defined by the following summation of products:

$$p = \sum_{i=1}^{n} \frac{\prod_{j=1}^{n}(x - x_j)_{j \neq i}}{\prod_{j=1}^{n}(x_i - x_j)_{j \neq i}} \qquad (2.1)$$

It can be shown by example that this approximation passes through all of the points, fitting exactly; therefore, it must be equal to the same polynomial of order **n-1** that you would get if you had performed a linear regression. While Lagrange interpolation can be useful, it can also yield wild variations between the data points, as illustrated in the following figure.

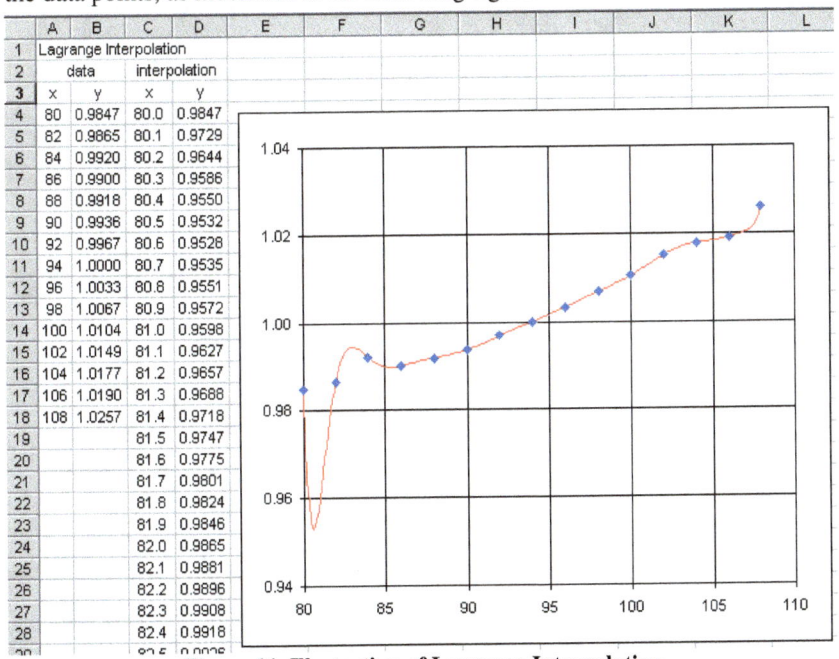

Figure 11. Illustration of Lagrange Interpolation

The code to implement Lagrange interpolation in VBA is listed below:

```
Function LagrangeInterpolation(X As Range, Y As Range,
ByVal Z As Double) As Double
  Dim i As Integer, j As Integer, P As Double
  LagrangeInterpolation = 0#
  For i = 1 To X.Count
    P = Y(i)
    For j = 1 To X.Count
      If (i <> j) Then
        P = P * (Z - X(j)) / (X(i) - X(j))
      End If
    Next j
    LagrangeInterpolation = LagrangeInterpolation + P
  Next i
End Function
```

The following code implements Lagrange interpolation in C:

```
double Lagrange(double*X,double*Y,int n,double x)
  {
  int i,j;
  double p,q;
  p=0.;
  for(i=0;i<n;i++)
    {
    q=Y[i];
    for(j=0;j<n;j++)
      if(j!=i)
        q*=(x-X[j])/(X[i]-X[j]);
    p+=q;
    }
  return(p);
  }
```

The code and data may be found in spreadsheet interpolation.xls.

Chapter 3. Cubic Splines

When you draw a *smoothed* line through data point with Excel® it uses a cubic spline to define the curve between the points. Cubic splines are generally well behaved compared to Lagrange interpolation (as described in Chapter 2), as the order never exceeds three, regardless of how many data points there are. The following figure illustrates this:

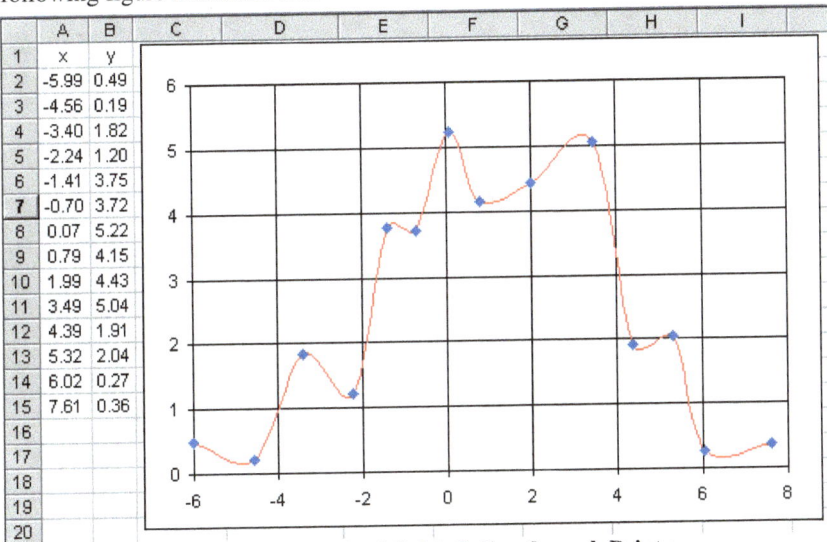

Figure 12. Example of Cubic Spline through Points

Though Excel™ will draw lines on a graph using cubic splines, it does not provide these as user-callable functions. Implementing a cubic spline as a VBA macro would be quite problematic and so this is instead done with an Add-In written in C, as described in Appendix A. A cubic spline is a series of third-order polynomials ($y=c_0+c_1x+c_2x^2+c_3x^3$) that match each of the data points exactly, plus have a continuous slope through each data point. As this these criteria imply four equations for each pair of points and there are four unknown coefficients (c_0 through c_3) in a third-order polynomial, the entire problem is defined. As long as the points are distinct, that is, no two are equal, the solution can be found. The following code creates and evaluates a cubic spline.

```
double*CreateSpline(double*X,double*Y,int n)
  {
  int i,k,l;
  double*C,d,q,t;
  if(n<2)
     return(NULL);
  for(i=1;i<n;i++)
     if(X[i]<=X[i-1])
        return(NULL);
```

```c
        if((C=calloc(3*n,sizeof(double)))==NULL)
           return(NULL);
        if(n==2)
           {
           C[0]=(Y[1]-Y[0])/(X[1]-X[0]);
           C[1]=0;
           C[2]=0;
           C[3]=C[0];
           C[4]=0;
           C[5]=0;
           return(C);
           }
        d=X[1]-X[0];
        C[2]=d;
        C[4]=(Y[1]-Y[0])/d;
        for(i=1;i<n-1;i++)
           {
           k=3*i;
           t=X[i+1]-X[i];
           C[k+2]=t;
           C[k]=2*(d+t);
           q=(Y[i+1]-Y[i])/t;
           C[k+4]=q;
           C[k+1]=q-C[k+1];
           d=t;
           }
        l=3*(n-1);
        C[0]=-C[2];
        C[l]=-C[l-1];
        C[1]=0;
        C[l+1]=0;
        if(n>3)
           {
           C[1]=C[7]/(X[3]-X[1])-C[4]/(X[2]-X[0]);
           C[l+1]=C[l-2]/(X[n-1]-X[n-3])-C[l-5]/(X[n-2]-X[n-
4]);
           C[1]=C[1]*C[2]*C[2]/(X[3]-X[0]);
           C[l+1]=-C[l+1]*C[l-1]*C[l-1]/(X[n-1]-X[n-4]);
           }
        for(i=1;i<n;i++)
           {
           k=3*i;
           t=C[k-1]/C[k-3];
           C[k]-=t*C[k-1];
           C[k+1]-=t*C[k-2];
           }
        C[l+1]=C[l+1]/C[l];
        for(i=n-1;i>0;i--)
           {
```

```
   k=3*(i-1);
   C[k+1]=(C[k+1]-C[k+2]*C[k+4])/C[k];
   }
 C[l]=(Y[n-1]-Y[n-2])/C[l-1]+C[l-1]*(C[l-2]+2*C[l+1]);
 for(i=0;i<n-1;i++)
   {
   k=3*i;
   C[k]=(Y[i+1]-Y[i])/C[k+2]-C[k+2]*(C[k+4]+2*C[k+1]);
   C[k+2]=(C[k+4]-C[k+1])/C[k+2];
   C[k+1]*=3;
   }
 C[l+1]*=3;
 C[l+2]=C[l-1];
 return(C);
 }
double EvaluateSpline(double*X,double*Y,int n,double*C,double x,int m)
 {
 int i,i1,i2,k,n1;
 if(n<2)
    return(0.);
 n1=n-1;
 if(x<=X[0])
    i=0;
 else if(x>=X[n1])
    i=n1;
 else
    {
    i1=0;
    i2=n1;
    for(k=0;k<32;k++)
       {
       i=(i1+i2)/2;
       if(x<X[i]||i==n1)
          i2=i;
       else if(x>X[i+1])
          i1=i;
       else
          break;
       }
    }
 x-=X[i];
 k=3*i;
 if(m==1)
    return((3*C[k+2]*x+2*C[k+1])*x+C[k]);
 if(m==2)
    return(6*C[k+2]*x+2*C[k+1]);
 if(m==3)
    return(6*C[k+2]);
```

```
    return(((C[k+2]*x+C[k+1])*x+C[k])*x+Y[i]);
  }
```

You call procedure CreateSpline() once and receive a pointer to an array of coefficients then procedure EvaluateSpline() as many times as desired to use the spline. The evaluator for this particular implementation will return the value as well as the first, second, or third derivative, which can be quite useful. Note that the evaluator uses the same bisection search [for(k=0;k<32;k++) above] as the previous enhanced linear interpolation macro to speed things up when many points are used.

Chapter 4. Bisection Search

The Newton-Raphson and Secant methods are most often recommended for solving nonlinear equations in one variable, such as $x=\ln(1/x)$, $x=?$. While these methods may be adequate and even rapid, they don't always work. In some cases and for some equations, these methods can result in wild oscillations and even errors that will lock up a spreadsheet. In contrast, the bisection method always yields a result to whatever level of accuracy is required, as long as the equation satisfies the requirement of always increasing or decreasing but not both.

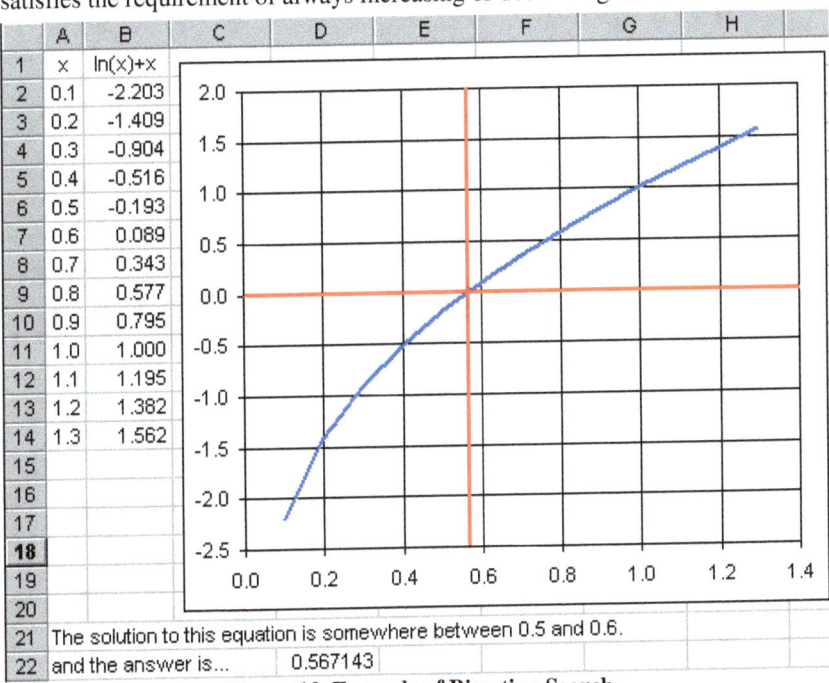

Figure 13. Example of Bisection Search

We begin our bisections with a lower and upper bound. The solution can be anywhere between these two values. Each time we calculate and compare, replacing either the lower or upper bound so that the interval decreases by half. The accuracy is $1/2^n$, where n is the number of bisections. 32 iterations achieve one part in 4 billion. A VBA macro to implement this approach is listed below:

```
Function Bisection(target As Double) As Double
   Dim iter As Integer, x1 As Double, x2 As Double
   x1 = -3
   x2 = 3
   For iter = 1 To 32
      Bisection = (x1 + x2) / 2
      If (Y(Bisection) < target) Then
         x1 = Bisection
```

```
        Else
            x2 = Bisection
        End If
    Next iter
End Function
```

An example containing data, graph, and code may be found in the online archive in folder examples and spreadsheet bisection_search.xls.

Chapter 5. Secant Method

There is one problem where I always deploy the secant method: finding density (ρ) from pressure for steam and other fluids. Each evaluation is time-consuming due to the complexity of the equations involved. The bisection method would require 32 iterations and I would like to get this down to 8 or even 4. The Newton-Raphson method requires knowledge of the derivative, or $\partial p/\partial \rho$, which would be even more time-consuming. This makes the secant method the most attractive. The Newton-Raphson method can be expressed by:

$$x_{n+1} = x_n + \frac{y(x_n)}{\left(\dfrac{dy}{dx}\right)_{x_n}} \qquad (5.1)$$

where n and n+1 are the current and next iterative values. From the definition of the derivative, we get:

$$\frac{dy}{dx} \approx \frac{y_2 - y_1}{x_2 - x_1} \qquad (5.2)$$

and so we use this approximation to formulate an iterative step:

$$x_3 = \frac{x_1 y_2 - x_2 y_1}{y_2 - y_1} \qquad (5.3)$$

here the subscripts 1, 2, and 3 indicate the previous two values and the next step, respectively. This method will run into trouble whenever $y_2 \approx y_1$, and so we carefully avoid this when choosing a starting sequence. The following code implements this approach:

```
rho1=first estimate
rho2=second estimate
p1=pressure(T,rho1);
p2=pressure(T,rho2);
for(i=0;i<32;i++)
  {
  if(fabs(p2-p1)<p/1E7)
    break;
  rho3=(rho1*(p2-p)-rho2*(p1-p))/(p2-p1);
  p3=pressure(T,rho3);
  if(fabs(p3/p-1.)<0.0001)
    break;
  if(fabs(p1-p)<fabs(p2-p))
    {
    rho2=rho3;
    p2=p3;
    }
  else
```

```
        {
        rho1=rho3;
        p1=p3;
        }
    }
    return(rho3);
```
The first if() statement above tests for convergence by virtue of agreement with the target and the second by collapse of the interval. The third and fourth if() statements avoid collapse of the denominator in Equation 5.3. Tests for steam show that on average 3½ iterations are required or about $1/10^{th}$ the effort of a bisection search. I can't remember the last time I used the Newton-Raphson method.

Chapter 6. Using the Excel™ Solver

Excel's Solver is quite useful. It works very much like the Newton-Raphson method and, in fact, may apply this method based on the options selected. While it is possible to implement the Solver within a macro inside a spreadsheet, launching it multiple times, it is most often used once; that is, to solve one specific problem. If you have not used this before, you will have to specifically enable it. See Excel's help for how to do this for your particular version. Excel™ also has a *goal seek* feature, which is similar, though nowhere near as useful.

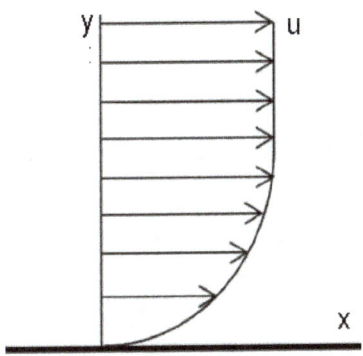

Figure 14. Boundary Layer

There are countless examples of how we might use the Solver. The example we consider here is the Blasius boundary layer equation. This problem arises in fluid mechanics and involves solving partial differential equations for flow over a flat plate (illustrated above). The detail we are interested in here is finding the value of the second partial of the velocity with respect to distance from the wall ($\partial^2 u/\partial x^2$) at the wall ($x=0$) such that the first partial ($\partial u/\partial x$) far away from the wall is exactly 1. The details may be found in the online archive in folder examples and spreadsheet blasius.xls. More details on boundary layers and the Blasius equation in particular may be found on the web, for example:

https://en.wikipedia.org/wiki/Blasius_boundary_layer

We set up the calculations, which require a guess for the unknown (this goes in cell D3, shown in bold green type). We solve out to some large distance (in this case 10), where we check the value (in cell C103, shown in bold red type). Two methods (explicit and implicit Euler) are illustrated on two separate tabs. The outcome is the same but the methods and calculations may be of some interest for other problems. We then launch the Solver, set the target cell to C103 and the target value to 1.0, then set the adjustable parameter to cell D3 and press the Solve button. It's that simple.

The details of this example are shown in the following figure:

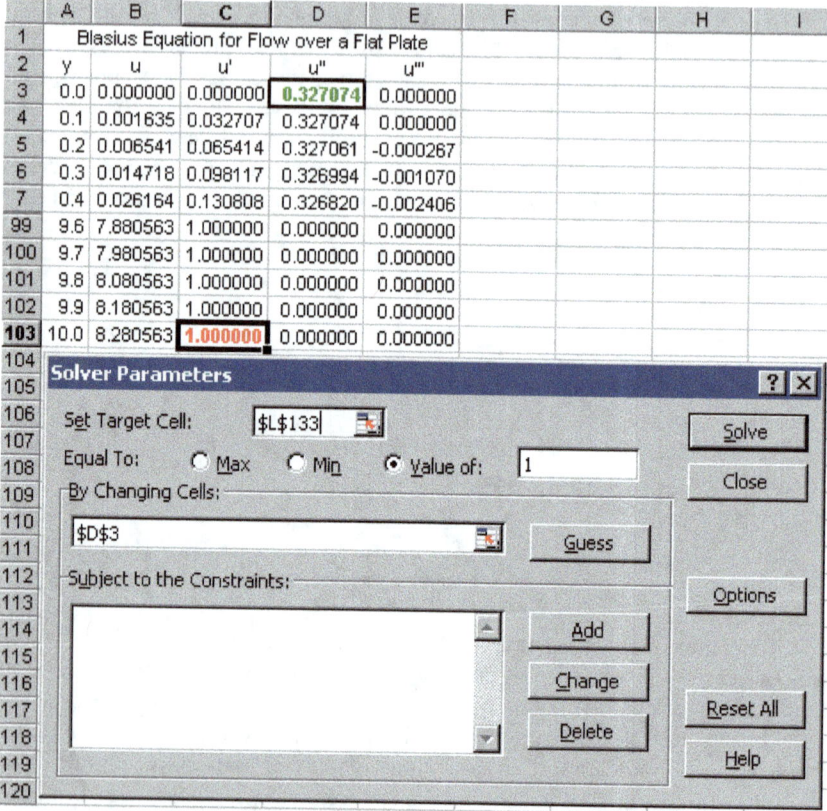

Figure 15. Illustration of Using the Excel™ Solver

This is but one example of the many problems you can solve using this tool. Not only will it solve nonlinear problems, it will solve them in more than one variable. As this works so well and is so convenient to set up, there is no point reinventing the wheel to solve this type of problem.

Chapter 7. Using Excel's LINEST

Excel's LINEST (linear estimation) function can be quite useful. It finds one or more coefficients that combine in a linear sum applied to columns of independent variables to best approximate a single column of dependent values. While the combination is linear ($y=c_1f_1+c_2f_2+c_3f_3...$) this does not mean that the functions appearing in the independent columns (f_1, f_2, f_3, ...) need be linear. These can be as simple as x, x^2, x^3, ... or more complex, such as $sin(x^2)$, $exp(x)$, etc. Here we will use LINEST to solve a common problem, which can be reduced to a second order polynomial expansion in two variables, namely: $z=c_0+c_1x+c_2y+c_3x^2+c_4xy+c_5y^2$. The problem is one of fitting a family of curves supplied by a manufacturer for a typical water-cooled steam surface condenser at a large coal-fired power plant. The curves provided by the manufacturer are shown below:

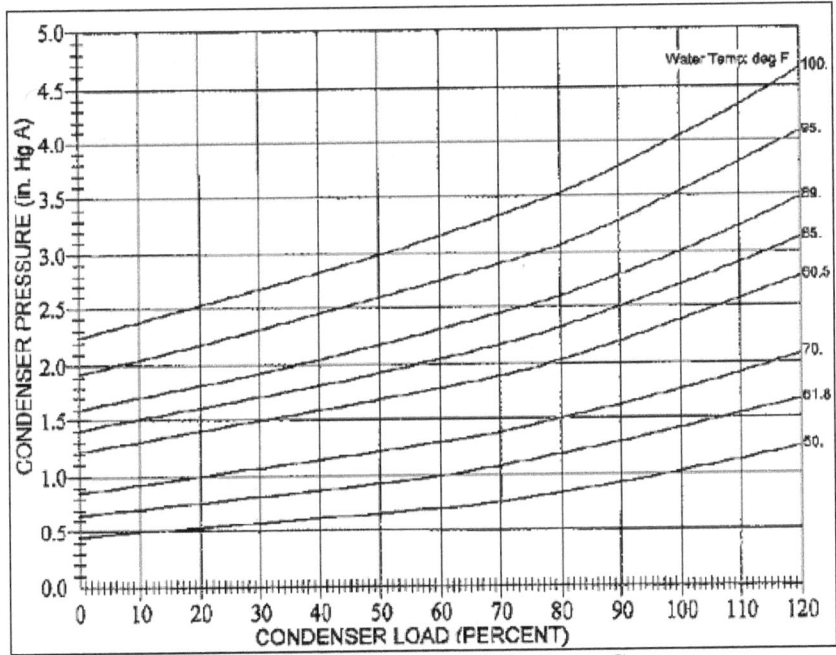

Figure 16. Typical Water-Cooled Condenser Curves

We first digitize the curves. This is most often done with specialized software designed for this task. Such a program (Digitize) can be downloaded for free at the link below the Preface. The horizontal (X) axis is condenser heat load (or *duty*) in percent. Before we set up the regression, we recognize that this is a heat exchanger and that the process (heat transfer) is driven by temperature (and not pressure) differences so that the underlying performance is should be a temperature correlation. Next we set up the dependent variables, in this case: *Tin*, *duty*, Tin^2, $Tin \times duty$, and $duty^2$.

	A	B	C	D	E	F	G	H
1	Typical Water-Cooled Condenser Curves							
2	digitized curves			expansion of variables			target	fit
3	pres.	Tin	duty	Tin^2	duty*Tin	duty^2	Tsat	Tsat
4	in.Hg	°F	%	°F^2	%°F	%^{2}	°F	°F
5	0.46	50.0	0%	2500	0.01	0.000	56.3	55.9
6	0.50	50.0	10%	2500	5.13	0.011	58.9	58.0
7	0.53	50.0	20%	2500	10.02	0.040	60.4	60.0
8	0.58	50.0	30%	2500	15.07	0.091	62.8	62.1
9	0.61	50.0	40%	2500	20.04	0.161	64.6	64.3
10	0.66	50.0	50%	2500	25.08	0.252	66.7	66.6
11	0.70	50.0	60%	2500	30.13	0.363	68.2	69.0
12	0.75	50.0	70%	2500	35.10	0.493	70.5	71.4
13	0.83	50.0	80%	2500	40.07	0.642	73.5	74.0
14	0.92	50.0	90%	2500	45.03	0.811	76.6	76.6

Figure 17. Curve Data and Input Columns for LINEST

Column A contains the pressure off the vertical (Y) axis of the manufacturer's curves. Column B contains the inlet water temperatures (one for each curve, listed on the right side). Column C contains the heat load (duty) or horizontal (X) axis. Columns D, E, and F contain Tin^2, $Tin \times duty$, and $duty^2$, respectively. Columns B through F (are contiguous for convenience) and form the 5 independent variables for the regression. Column G is saturation temperature of steam corresponding to the pressure from column A. A curve-fit for steam saturation pressure and temperature are provided as VBA macros inside the spreadsheet (condenser.xls), which may be found in the examples folder. LINEST is called (inputs and outputs) in cells I2:N6, as shown below:

	I	J	K	L	M	N
1	LINEST					
2	4.107	-0.06	0.001	22.35	0.783	13.29
3	0.304	0.006	2E-04	0.624	0.025	0.949
4	1	0.384	#N/A	#N/A	#N/A	#N/A
5	43079	98	#N/A	#N/A	#N/A	#N/A
6	31751	14.45	#N/A	#N/A	#N/A	#N/A

Figure 18. Input/Output Cells for LINEST

From Excel's help, you will find a description of the contents of these cells:

	A	B	C	D	E	F
1	m_n	m_{n-1}	...	m_2	m_1	b
2	se_n	se_{n-1}	...	se_2	se_1	se_b
3	r^2	se_y				
4	F	d_f				
5	ss_{reg}	ss_{resid}				

Figure 19. Excerpt from Excel Help

The most important cells are A1:F2 (in the help file or I2:N2 in our spreadsheet), which contain the coefficients in reverse order. Cell A3 (or I4) contains the regression coefficient, R^2, cell A4 (or I5) contains the F-value, and A5 (or I6) contains the sum of the residuals squared (i.e., the total error in the regression). See any text on regression for an explanation of these terms. We use the results of the regression to calculate column H:

```
H5=N$2+M$2*B5+L$2*C5+K$2*D5+J$2*E5+I$2*F5
```

The $2 after N, M, L, K, J, and I lock in row 2. We see how good the regression is (in transform variable, Tsat) in this next figure:

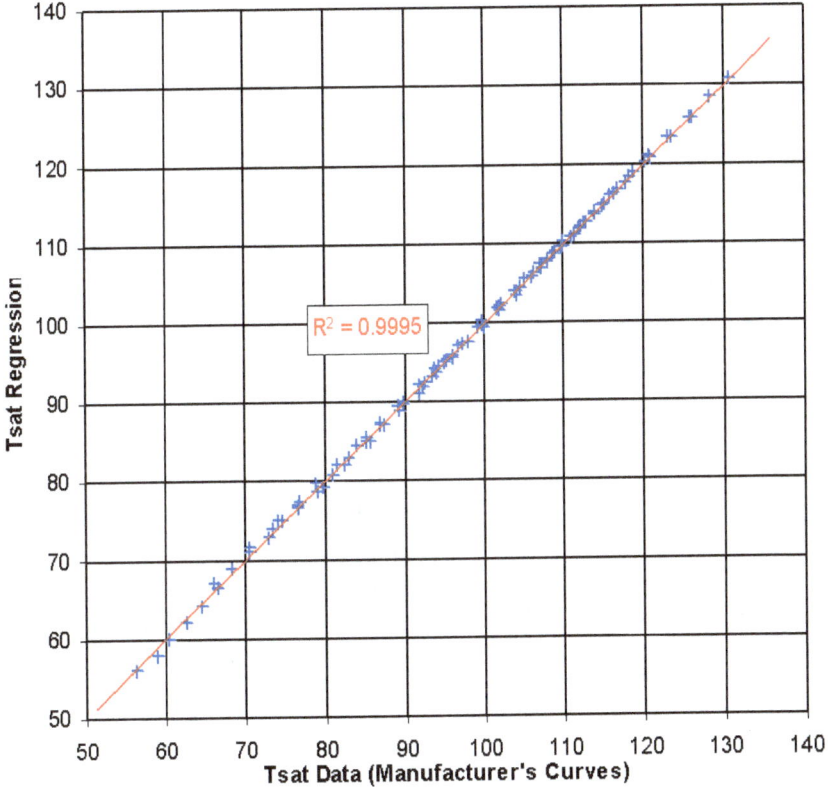

Figure 20. Regression Agreement (Goodness of Fit)

We see how well the original curves are reproduced by our regression in this next figure:

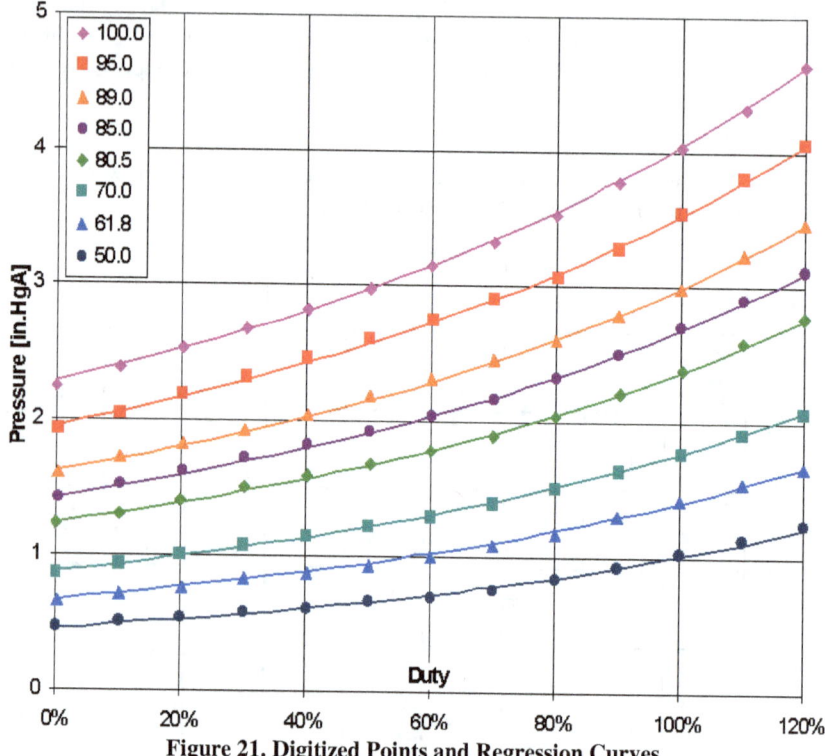

Figure 21. Digitized Points and Regression Curves

Combining Solver and LINEST

Before we leave this section of using Excel's features, a combination I often use to great advantage uses the Solver *and* LINEST together. There is a class of curves (generator and also transformer losses) that are linear and nonlinear. That is, one nonlinear term will reduce an entire family of curves to a single curve, which we can then determine using LINEST. We use Solver to find the parameter that results in the best linear fit. We set up as for the condenser curves with an estimate of the nonlinear parameter, then fine-tune it. We can either maximize the regression coefficient, R^2, or minimize the sum of the squares of the residual. While either will often work, sometimes one works better than the other. In the example we solve here, it works better to maximize R^2.

The following are typical generator loss curves supplied by the manufacturer. The horizontal (X) axis is net generator output in megawatts. The vertical (Y) axis is generator loss in kilowatts (an X:Y factor of 1000:1). The curves are at four values (1.00, 0.95, 0.90, and 0.85) of power factor, which is a measure of the alignment (synchronization) in time of the voltage and current. This is a 3-phase generator, such as one would find at a large plant supplying power to the grid. Lower load (power draw) on the grid is usually accompanied by a power factor closer to unity (1), while greater load is usually accompanied by a smaller power factor (perhaps 0.85 or less).

The trick to fitting these generator (and also transformer) curves is recognizing that were we to plot loss vs. net power/power factor raised to some exponent (net/PF^n), the four curves (as well as similar ones for 0.80, 0.75, etc.) will collapse to a single curve. Then we use LINEST to fit a curve through that. First, we must find that special exponent, which is a nonlinear problem. As it turns out, the exponent will be somewhere between 0.5 and 2.5, depending on the design of the generator or transformer; thus we start with a value of 1. We set the spreadsheet (generator.xls) up as before with the digitized data. Instead of filling the columns with x, x^2, and x^3 we use a shortcut notation:

=LINEST(C3:C79,D3:D79^{1,2,3},TRUE,TRUE)

The single x column is D3:D79. We instruct Excel™ to create two more virtual columns with ^{1,2,3}. We could use 1,3,5 or something similar, but the syntax is otherwise limited; that is, we can't specify exp(x) or sin(x) this way.

A	B	C	D	E	F	G	H	I
1	Typical Generator Loss Curves				LINEST			
2	PF	kWnet	kWloss	1.5048	fit	-37.7215	917.146	20.16417	774.1076
3	0.85	1,183	772	0.0068	774	45.444	84.00668	43.45553	6.096061
4	0.85	14,201	786	0.0819	782	0.998547	15.10124	#N/A	#N/A
5	0.85	33,728	826	0.1945	812	16718.52	73	#N/A	#N/A
6	0.85	53,254	878	0.3072	866	11437839	16647.45	#N/A	#N/A

Figure 22. Spreadsheet Setup Data and Regression

The exponent (1.5048) is in cell D2. It is initially 1, then optimized by the Solver to achieve the maximum R^2 in cell F4, as shown below:

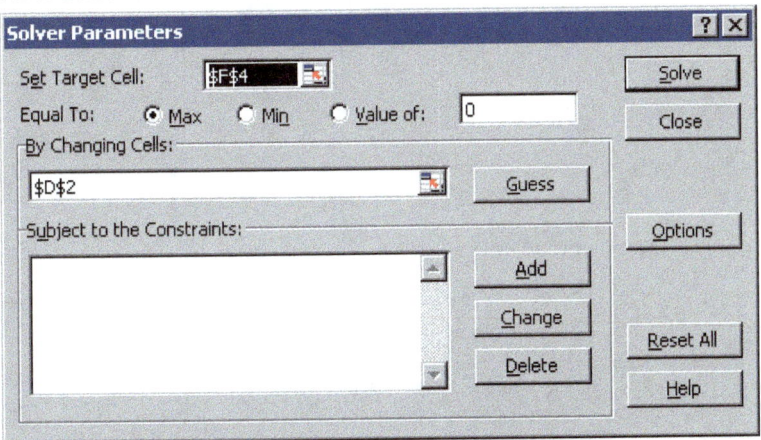

Figure 23. Solver Setup for Generator Example

We see the agreement between data and regression in this next figure:

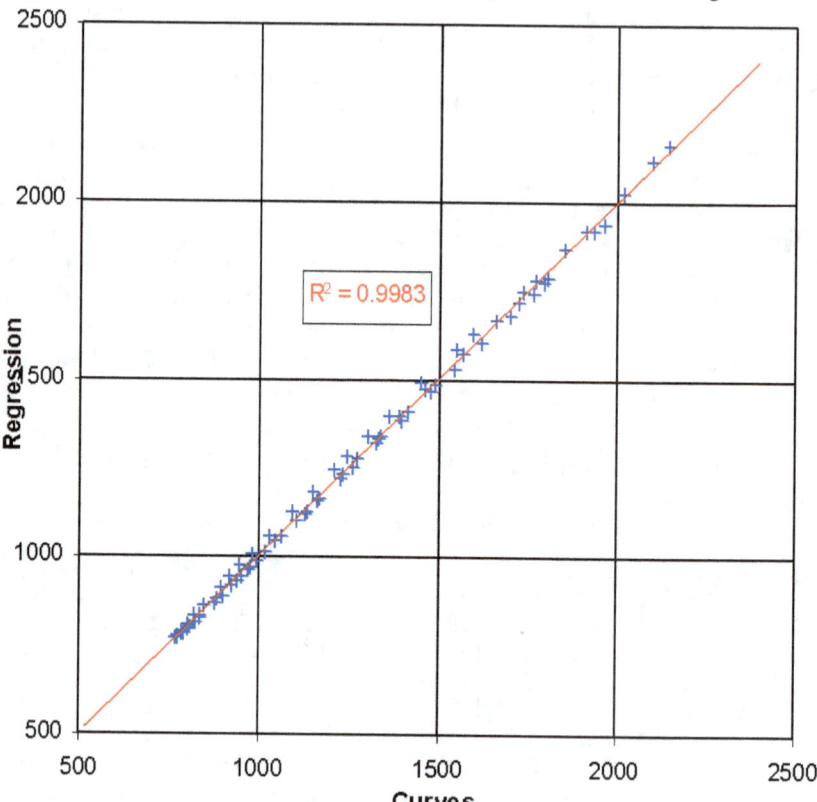

Figure 24. Agreement with Data for Generator Example

The final curves agree quite well with the manufacturer's and can also be used at some distance outside the original range of 0.85 to 1.00, which is useful because manufacturers often are reluctant to provide curves outside this range, as these imply a guarantee.

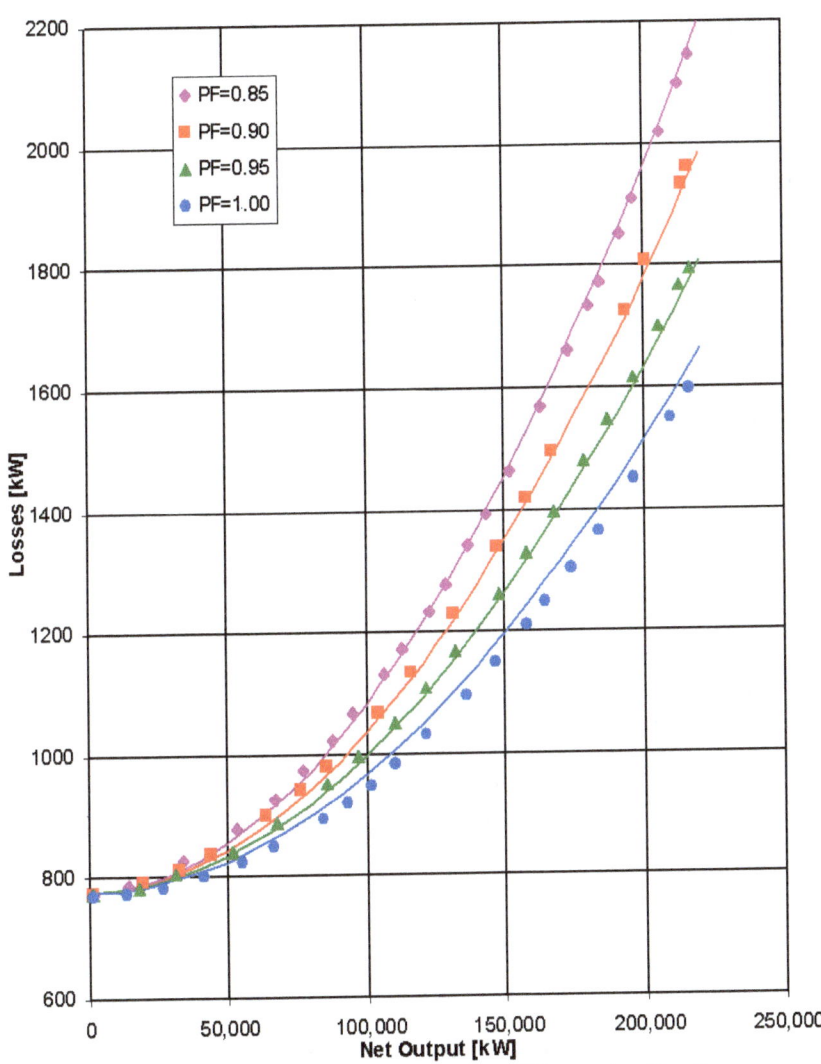

Figure 25. Generator Digitized Points and Regression Results

Least-Squares vs. Min/Max

Presentations of curve-fitting, regression, or optimization almost always emphasize the least-square residual; that is, the sum of the squares of the residuals or errors. But there is another way... Before we consider this alternative, we will consider how the traditional approach is derived. Consider an approximating polygon of order n-1: $p(x)=c_0+c_1x+c_2x^2+c_3x^3+...$ We know the value at several points $(x_1, x_2, x_3, ...)$, say m, where $m \geq n$. The residuals $(r_1=y_1-p(x_1), r_2=y_2-p(x_2), ...)$ can be represented by the following matrix operation:

$$R = B - AC \qquad (7.1)$$

where R and B have m rows and 1 column, A has m rows and n columns, and C has n rows and 1 column. Matrix B contains the values of $y1, y2, y3, ...$, C contains $c0, c1, c2, ...$, and A contains:

$$A = \begin{bmatrix} 1 & x_1 & x_1^2 & x_1^3 \\ 1 & x_2 & x_2^2 & x_2^3 \\ 1 & x_3 & x_3^2 & x_3^3 \\ 1 & x_n & x_n^2 & x_n^3 \end{bmatrix} \qquad (7.2)$$

Matrix A is called a Vandermonde. The sum-square residual is:

$$residual = \sum_{i=1}^{m} r_i^2 \qquad (7.3)$$

which is equal to:

$$\sum_{i=1}^{m} r_i^2 = R^T R \qquad (7.4)$$

Performing the transpose and multiplication in Equation 7.4 on Equation 7.1 yields:

$$R^T R = A^T C^T CA - 2A^T C^T B + B^T B \qquad (7.5)$$

The minimum residual is found by differentiating Equation 7.5 by the coefficients, C, which yields:

$$A^T AC = A^T B \qquad (7.6)$$

The values of C which yield the least sum squared residual are then given by:

$$C = \left[A^T A\right]^{-1} \left[A^T B\right] \qquad (7.7)$$

This is what the Excel™ LINEST function does for you (and also the C code provided in matrix.c). This process considers the squares, which means that all of the residuals contribute to this objective. But what if we're most interested in the biggest discrepancy, not all the little discrepancies? That's call the min/max or the approximation that achieves the minimum, maximum error. We could accomplish this using the Excel™ Solver feature by initializing the coefficients of our approximation using LINEST, calculating the residuals at every point, creating a cell with an appropriate equation so that it contains the largest discrepancy, and configuring the Solver to minimize that cell. This is essentially what we've already done with the generator curves. You will find a spreadsheet in the archive, minmax.xls, which contains two examples. One is shown below:

	A	B	C	D	E	F	G	H	I	J	K	L
1	data		least sq.		min/max		4th order	approximations				
2	x	y	fit	err	fit	err	least-squares	x	sq	mm		
3	-5.99	0.49	0.61	0.12	-0.56	1.05	4.491900028	-6.0	0.62	-0.55		
4	-4.56	0.19	0.15	0.04	-0.38	0.58	0.580399094	-5.9	0.51	-0.60		
5	-3.40	1.82	1.04	0.78	0.71	1.11	-0.21789963	-5.8	0.41	-0.64		
6	-2.24	1.20	2.36	1.16	2.10	0.90	-0.01543159	-5.7	0.32	-0.67		
7	-1.41	3.75	3.30	0.45	3.08	0.67	0.003181404	-5.6	0.25	-0.69		
8	-0.70	3.72	3.98	0.26	3.79	0.07	4th order	-5.5	0.19	-0.70		
9	0.07	5.22	4.53	0.69	4.39	0.83	min/max	-5.4	0.14	-0.70		
10	0.79	4.15	4.81	0.66	4.73	0.58	4.345230041	-5.3	0.10	-0.69		
11	1.99	4.43	4.71	0.28	4.78	0.35	0.655767257	-5.2	0.08	-0.67		
12	3.49	5.04	3.68	1.36	3.94	1.10	-0.19945184	-5.1	0.06	-0.65		
13	4.39	1.91	2.72	0.81	3.02	1.12	-0.01463946	-5.0	0.06	-0.62		
14	5.32	2.04	1.64	0.40	1.88	0.16	0.002358918	-4.9	0.07	-0.57		
15	6.02	0.27	0.90	0.63	0.97	0.70		-4.8	0.08	-0.53		
16	7.61	0.36	0.16	0.20	-0.76	1.12		-4.7	0.11	-0.47		
17			max=	1.36	≥	1.12		-4.6	0.14	-0.41		
18			sumsq=	6.32	≤	9.31		-4.5	0.18	-0.34		

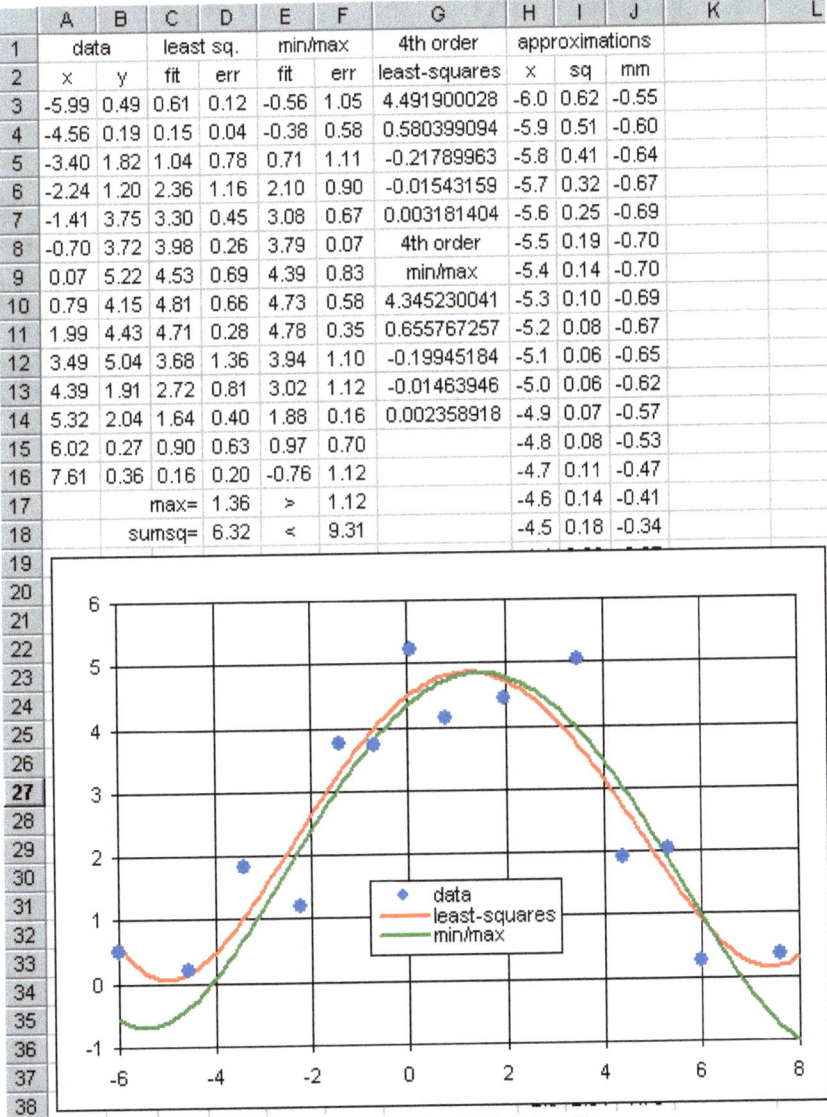

Figure 26. Example of Min/Max Fit

29

Through a very convoluted derivation, it can be shown that the min/max fit is obtained when the approximation exactly matches the data at a certain number of points. The question then becomes, which points? Various algorithms exist for swapping nodes, fitting, evaluating, and keeping track of the best one. If we had to try every possible combination, this would take an unreasonable amount of time. Fortunately, adequate results are often obtained by shuffling the selection of points around the ones with the largest residuals. A C code (minmax.c) is also provided that illustrates this process, though Excel's LINEST and Solver are convenient and usually adequate.

Chapter 8. Using qsort()

The C library function qsort() is quite useful but often programmers don't know how to effectively utilize this built-in capability, which isn't surprising because the syntax is abstruse (strangely complicated and often confusing). The key is creating a comparison function for your particular data type and structure. We consider several examples here. First, the simplest possible comparison: null-terminated strings. The comparison itself is easy enough, we use the library function strcmp() for a case-sensitive comparison or stricmp() for a case-insensitive comparison. The function we need is:

```
int CompareStrings(const void*a,const void*b)
{
return(_stricmp(*(char**)a,*(char**)b));
}
```

Note that the items enter as constant void pointers, even through they never are constant or pointers to a void. If these were literally constants, we couldn't sort them. If they were voids, there would be no point in sorting them. We must strong type these using *(char**). Do not get lazy and use (char*), as this may not work and may even crash. We initiate the sort with the following call:

```
qsort((void*)list,n,sizeof(char*),CompareStrings);
```

Here the list is a char** or an array of char*; that is, an array of pointers to null-terminated strings. The code and example, including a list of the 87 most populous cities, can be found in the examples folder in qsort.c. This file also contains the public domain version of qsort written by Ray Gardner, should you want to see how the qsort is implemented. We will not cover the theory behind the "quick" sort in this text. Discussions are readily available on the Web.

Next we sort alphabetically by country and then by city. This requires a slightly more complicated user-defined comparison function. We first define a structure to contain the data:

```
typedef struct{char*name,*country;int population;}CITY;
/* World's 87 Largest Cities by Population */
CITY cities[]={
  {"Chongqing"    ,"China"   ,28846170},
  {"Shanghai"     ,"China"   ,23019148},
  {"Beijing"      ,"China"   ,19612368},
  etc...
  {NULL           ,NULL      ,       0}};
```

The comparison must be a two-step process. We use the same string comparison (strcmp or stricmp) for both, but we want to call this as few times as possible.

```
int CompareByCountry(const void*a,const void*b)
    {
    int k;
    k=_stricmp(((CITY*)a)->country,((CITY*)b)->country);
    if(k!=0)
        return(k);
    return(_stricmp(((CITY*)a)->name,((CITY*)b)->name));
    }
```

First we compare countries and get the result into the integer k. If k is not zero, then we return the value. If k is zero, we go on to compare the cities. Regardless of the outcome (say there are two cities with the same name), we return, so there is no point in using k=... return(k). The simple return(_stricmp) is more efficient. Next, we will sort by country and then by population and finally by city. That comparison is:

```
int CompareByCountryAndPopulation(const void*a,const void*b)
    {
    int k;
    k=_stricmp(((CITY*)a)->country,((CITY*)b)->country);
    if(k!=0)
        return(k);
    k=(((CITY*)a)->population)-(((CITY*)b)->population);
    if(k!=0)
        return(k);
    return(_stricmp(((CITY*)a)->name,((CITY*)b)->name));
    }
```

The central (second) comparison will result in a sort from low to high (smallest first, largest last). To reverse this (largest to smallest), swap a and b, as shown below:

```
        k=(((CITY*)b)->population)-(((CITY*)a)->population);
```

This same process can be modified for other data objects, for example if you wanted to sort data by time. If the time is a floating-point number, a simple difference (k=t1-t2) won't work, as t1 and t2 aren't integers. While you could make multiple decisions based on processor flags (less than, greater than, equal, etc.), there is no way in code to obtain the needed result from a single test; therefore, we use something like the following:

```
int CompareData(const void*v1,const void*v2)
    {
    if((*(DATA*)v1).time<(*(DATA*)v2).time)
        return(-1);
    if((*(DATA*)v1).time>(*(DATA*)v2).time)
        return(1);
```

```
      return(0);
      }
```
If t1<t2, return −1. If t1>t2, return +1. Otherwise return zero. Used with qsort, this will arrange the data in order of increasing time. If we wanted to sort nodes (XYZ), we would use three paired comparisons:

```
typedef struct{double X,Y,Z;}NODE;
int CompareData(const void*v1,const void*v2)
    {
    if((*(NODE*)v1).X<(*(NODE*)v2).X)
       return(-1);
    if((*(NODE*)v1).X>(*(NODE*)v2).X)
       return(1);
    if((*(NODE*)v1).Y<(*(NODE*)v2).Y)
       return(-1);
    if((*(NODE*)v1).Y>(*(NODE*)v2).Y)
       return(1);
    if((*(NODE*)v1).Z<(*(NODE*)v2).Z)
       return(-1);
    if((*(NODE*)v1).Z>(*(NODE*)v2).Z)
       return(1);
    return(0);
    }
```

In these comparisons we can use (*(NODE*)v1).X to strong type convert the const void pointer to a NODE pointer, then to a NODE structure, then select the X, Y, or Z element. We could also use ((NODE*)v1)->X, which would strong type convert the const void pointer to a NODE pointer, then using that NODE pointer select the X, Y, or Z element. This is why I said at the beginning of this chapter that the syntax is abstruse. You should be able to use qsort to sort anything with the examples in qsort.c. Examples and code for sorting indexed items (integers, doubles, and RGBs) can be found in quicksort.c

Chapter 9. Insertion Sort

While sorting an existing list of items is often enough, sometimes we want to gather information, such as nodes and elements in a model. In that case we may want to build a growing list that is in order and only contains the unique values (e.g., removing duplicate points or nodes). The task becomes an insertion sort; that is, find out where the next item should go into the list. If there already is one, discard the new one. If not, insert it. While we could use the same node comparison function from the previous chapter, a straightforward local comparison is more direct and may be more efficient.

We will consider three variants: 1) the simplest possible comparison and insertion; 2) a bisection search with insertion; and 3) a separate list of pointers. The motivation for 2) is speed. We may have a million nodes to consider and we don't want to initiate n^2 comparisons. The motivation for 3) is also speed. If we must move the objects around many, many times and they are large, it makes more sense to create a list of pointers to the objects and simply move the pointers.

First, we consider the simplest example: building a list of real numbers. The code may be found in the online archive in the examples folder in file insert.c. The insertion function is listed below:

```
void InsertPoint(double p)
  {
  int i;
  if(list.m==0)
    {
    list.m=10;
    if((list.d=calloc(list.m,sizeof(double)))==NULL)
      {
      printf("can't allocate memory for points\n");
      exit(1);
      }
    list.d[0]=p;
    list.n=1;
    return;
    }
  for(i=0;i<list.n;i++)
    {
    if(list.d[i]<p)
      continue;
    if(list.d[i]>p)
      break;
    return;
    }
  if(list.n>=list.m)
    {
    double*t=list.d;
    list.m+=10;
```

```
    if((list.d=calloc(list.m,sizeof(double)))==NULL)
      {
      printf("can't allocate memory for points\n");
      exit(1);
      }
    memcpy(list.d,t,list.n*sizeof(double));
    free(t);
    }
  if(i<list.n)
    memmove(list.d+i+1,list.d+i,
      (list.n-i)*sizeof(double));
  list.d[i]=p;
  list.n++;
  }
```

In this example we pass the function a list and number of points. We write the function to handle any number, not presuming this to be many or few. We initially create space for 10, though this could be 1000 or more. We enter the first point and set the counter to 1. Then we loop through all of the points, either inserting them or discarding duplicates. We use a simple loop, for(j=0;j<k;j++), to find the location within the list where the current point fits. If it is unique, before we can add it, we must check to see if there is room: if(k>=m). If we need more space, we must create a new list, copy the old one into it, and then delete (free) the old list.

If the new point is at the end, we simply add it. If it is inside if(j<k) then we must open up a gap for it. For this we use memmove. Do not use memcpy, as the addresses overlap and you will overwrite part of the existing list. The memmove instruction is specifically designed to handle this. There is also no point copying or moving real numbers, strings, or other complex data structures. The functions in the standard include file memory.h (also included by string.h and malloc.h) perform byte operations and use machine instructions most efficiently to do so.

What if there are a million data points? The 2 nested loops for(i=1;i<n;i++) and for(j=0;j<k;j++) will result in an order n^2 comparison process, which we don't want; therefore, we use a bisection search. The same concept introduced in Chapter 4 is used here to reduce this from n^2 to no more than 16n or less. The modified function can be found in the same file and is listed below:

```
    void BisectPoint(double p)
      {
      int i,j,j1,j2,k;
      if(list.m==0)
        {
        list.m=10;
        if((list.d=calloc(list.m,sizeof(double)))==NULL)
          {
          printf("can't allocate memory for points\n");
          exit(1);
```

```
      }
   list.d[0]=p;
   list.n=1;
   return;
   }
j1=0;
j2=list.n;
for(i=0;i<32;i++)
   {
   j=(j1+j2)/2;
   k=compare(p,list.d[j]);
   if(k==0)
      return;
   if(j1==j)
      {
      if(k>0)
         j++;
      break;
      }
   else if(k>0)
      j1=j;
   else
      j2=j;
   }
if(list.n>=list.m)
   {
   double*t=list.d;
   list.m+=10;
   if((list.d=calloc(list.m,sizeof(double)))==NULL)
      {
      printf("can't allocate memory for points\n");
      exit(1);
      }
   memcpy(list.d,t,list.n*sizeof(double));
   free(t);
   }
if(j<list.n)
   memmove(list.d+j+1,list.d+j,
      (list.n-j)*sizeof(double));
list.d[j]=p;
list.n++;
}
```

This is very similar to the previous algorithm with the addition of j1=0, j2=list.n, for(i=0;i<32;i++) j=(j1+j2)/2, which is the same sequence used for the bisection search in solving a nonlinear equation, only here we're using integers to enter a list. Because we intend to use the test condition (<0,=0,>0) more than once, we use a function (compare(p,q)). For a more complex data structure, we could use the same comparison as in the previous chapter with qsort. As these are integers and 32 bisections would span 4,294,967,296 of them, we will run out of possibilities long before this upper limit. We must check (j==j1) because, if it does, our bisection has reached the end and so we exit the loop. The rest is the same as before.

Our last example in this chapter will be using a bisection search to perform an insertion sort on an indexed list of data structures. This is also in the same code (insert.c). First, we define the NODE structure, a structure (heap) to contain the list, and the comparison (very similar to the previous one):

```
typedef struct{double x,y,z;}NODE;
struct{int*l,m,n;NODE*node;}heap;
int CompareNodes(NODE p,NODE q)
   {
   if(p.x<q.x)
      return(-1);
   if(p.x>q.x)
      return(1);
   if(p.y<q.y)
      return(-1);
   if(p.y>q.y)
      return(1);
   if(p.z<q.z)
      return(-1);
   if(p.z>q.z)
      return(1);
   return(0);
   }
```

Then we define the insertion function:

```
void BisectNode(NODE p)
   {
   int i,j,j1,j2,k;
   if(heap.m==0)
      {
      heap.m=10;
      if((heap.l=calloc(heap.m,sizeof(int)))==NULL)
         {
         printf("can't allocate memory for points\n");
         exit(1);
         }
      if((heap.node=calloc(heap.m,sizeof(NODE)))==NULL)
         {
         printf("can't allocate memory for points\n");
         exit(1);
         }
      heap.node[0]=p;
      heap.l[0]=0;
      heap.n=1;
      return;
```

```
      }
    j1=0;
    j2=heap.n;
    for(i=0;i<32;i++)
       {
       j=(j1+j2)/2;
       k=CompareNodes(p,heap.node[heap.l[j]]);
       if(k==0)
          return;
       if(j1==j)
          {
          if(k>0)
             j++;
          break;
          }
       else if(k>0)
          j1=j;
       else
          j2=j;
       }
    if(heap.n>=heap.m)
       {
       int*l=heap.l;
       NODE*t=heap.node;
       heap.m+=10;
       if((heap.l=calloc(heap.m,sizeof(int)))==NULL)
          {
          printf("can't allocate memory for points\n");
          exit(1);
          }
       memcpy(heap.l,l,heap.n*sizeof(int));
       free(l);
       if((heap.node=calloc(heap.m,sizeof(NODE)))==NULL)
          {
          printf("can't allocate memory for points\n");
          exit(1);
          }
       memcpy(heap.node,t,heap.n*sizeof(NODE));
       free(t);
       }
    if(j<heap.n)
       memmove(heap.l+j+1,heap.l+j,(heap.n-j)*sizeof(int));
    heap.l[j]=heap.n;
    heap.node[heap.n]=p;
    heap.n++;
    }
```

We use the same bisection search as before. We must allocate space for the nodes and also the index into the list of nodes (int*heap.l). After finding the right location, we insert a gap, and put the index into the list, which is always the current number of nodes (heap.n). We then add the node at the end of the list of nodes (heap.node[heap.n]=p). We only use memmove (the slowest operation when there are a lot of elements) on the index, not the nodes, which might be very large data structures in some cases. This combines the two time-saving features (bisection search and indexed list).

Chapter 10. Test for Inside Polygon

This simple operation is needed in many applications. The example we will use here is points on a map. The data set we will use comes from the National Oceanographic and Atmospheric Administration (NOAA) National Climate Data Center (NCDC) Global Surface Summary of the Day (GSOD). This currently contains 29,591 meteorological stations. The data may be found here:

ftp://ftp.ncdc.noaa.gov/pub/data/gsod/

The stations and this example may be found in the online archive in the examples folder in spreadsheet meteorological_stations.xls, shown below:

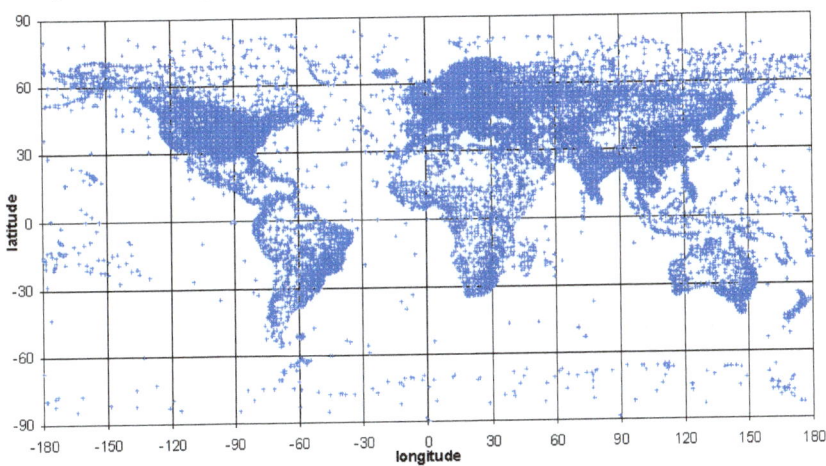

Figure 27. GSOD Meteorological Stations

We next consider polygons defining geographical areas:

Figure 28. Global Borders and Rivers

The test for inside polygon is basically a perimeter test for every point on the polygon either above or below and also left or right, keeping track of the cumulative logical tests. The VBA code is listed below:

```
Function InsidePolygon(xp As Range, yp As Range,
    x As Double, y As Double) As Boolean
  Dim above1 As Boolean, above2 As Boolean,
    i As Integer, iright As Integer
  Dim X1 As Double, X2 As Double, Y1 As Double,
    Y2 As Double
  iright = 0
  X2 = xp(xp.Count)
  Y2 = yp(xp.Count)
  If (Y2 > y) Then
    above2 = True
  Else
    above2 = False
  End If
  For i = 1 To xp.Count
    X1 = X2
    Y1 = Y2
    X2 = xp(i)
    Y2 = yp(i)
    above1 = above2
    If (Y2 > y) Then
      above2 = True
    Else
      above2 = False
    End If
    If (above1 <> above2) Then
      If (X1 > x And X2 > x) Then
        iright = iright + 1
      ElseIf (Y1 < Y2) Then
        If((x-X1)*(Y2-Y1)<(X2-X1)*(y-Y1))Then
          iright = iright + 1
        End If
      ElseIf(Y1>Y2)Then
        If((x-X1)*(Y2-Y1)>(X2-X1)*(y-Y1))Then
          iright = iright + 1
        End If
      End If
    End If
  Next i
  If (iright Mod 2 <> 0) Then
    InsidePolygon = True
  Else
    InsidePolygon = False
  End If
End Function
```

The polygon is presumed closed so the last point must not be the same as the first (it is implied) or the test will always fail. The "lower 48" polygon is shown below:

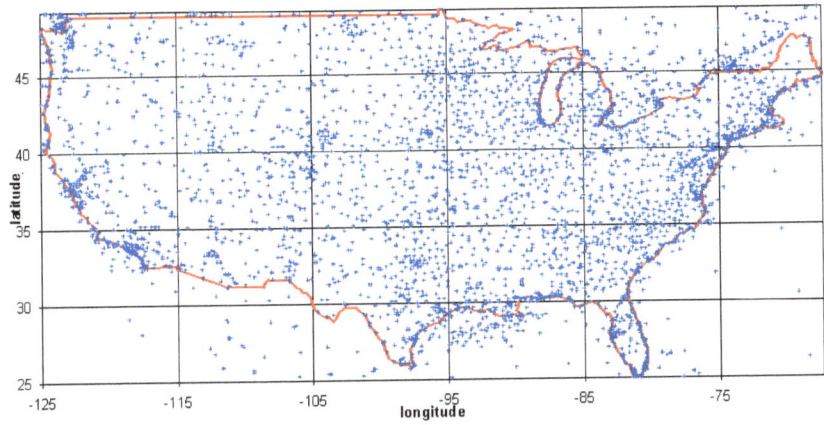

Figure 29. Lower 48 Polygon

The test is implemented in the spreadsheet as:

```
=InsidePolygon(U$3:U$505,V$3:V$505,E5,F5)
```

A typical section where the results of the inside polygon test can be seen is:

	A	B	C	D	E	F	G	H
1	World Meteorological Stations from NOAA/NCDC/GSOD							
2	USAF	WBAN	CTRY	STATE	LON	LAT	ELEV(m)	lower 48
17295	720358	53999	US	OK	-98.006	35.473	431.9	TRUE
17296	720359	23902	US	OK	-96.675	35.275	312.1	TRUE
17297	720361	63870	US	AL	-86.312	31.043	95.7	TRUE
17298	720362	63874	US	AL	-86.611	31.846	137.5	TRUE
17299	720363	63872	US	AL	-85.129	31.951	86.9	TRUE
17300	720365	24267	US	OR	-124.290	42.074	139.9	FALSE
17301	720365	99999	US	OR	-124.290	42.074	140	FALSE
17302	720366	63879	US	WV	-80.652	38.687	388.6	TRUE
17303	720366	99999	US	WV	-80.652	38.687	387.1	TRUE
17304	720367	54927	US	MN	-94.746	45.372	359.7	TRUE
17305	720367	99999	US	MN	-94.747	45.372	359.7	TRUE
17306	720368	54924	US	MN	-95.783	43.987	494.7	TRUE
17307	720369	04135	US	ID	-111.098	43.743	1898.6	TRUE
17308	720371	54850	US	MI	-85.593	41.960	251.2	TRUE
17309	720373	92824	US	FL	-82.164	28.000	46.9	TRUE
17310	720374	92825	US	FL	-82.449	27.916	2.4	TRUE
17311	720375	54844	US	MI	-83.743	46.007	202.7	FALSE
17312	720376	63880	US	AL	-86.256	34.229	314.6	TRUE

Figure 30. Results of Inside Polygon Test

The equivalent C code may be found in inside_polygon.c in the same folder. Typical results of the test are shown below:

```
-129.92   36.91 is NOT inside the lower 48
-118.40   44.26 is     inside the lower 48
 -94.90   34.40 is     inside the lower 48
-108.98   46.88 is     inside the lower 48
 -80.63   42.40 is NOT inside the lower 48
-119.55   45.77 is     inside the lower 48
 -87.37   35.41 is     inside the lower 48
-111.76   20.45 is NOT inside the lower 48
-124.52   30.93 is NOT inside the lower 48
-121.16   24.98 is NOT inside the lower 48
 -70.69   33.37 is NOT inside the lower 48
-122.86   20.14 is NOT inside the lower 48
-129.47   31.34 is NOT inside the lower 48
 -98.10   37.14 is     inside the lower 48
 -93.89   38.21 is     inside the lower 48
-120.03   39.89 is     inside the lower 48
-102.95   30.56 is     inside the lower 48
-126.58   38.23 is NOT inside the lower 48
 -83.00   44.08 is     inside the lower 48
 -98.81   29.06 is     inside the lower 48
 -77.44   41.80 is     inside the lower 48
 -72.65   47.77 is NOT inside the lower 48
 -97.64   24.27 is NOT inside the lower 48
-102.28   27.06 is NOT inside the lower 48
 -78.27   26.29 is NOT inside the lower 48
 -83.22   45.31 is NOT inside the lower 48
 -70.19   49.99 is NOT inside the lower 48
 -93.31   31.77 is     inside the lower 48
-114.03   28.92 is NOT inside the lower 48
 -79.59   20.71 is NOT inside the lower 48
```

Chapter 11. Inverse Distance Interpolation

The inverse distance interpolation method is one of the most useful techniques for interpolating data, especially spatially disperse and even more so irregularly spaced. In short, the closer a known point is, the more influence it should have on the local (i.e., interpolated) value. Often a power of 2.5 is applied to the distance. This can be expressed by the following equation.

$$C = \frac{\sum \dfrac{C_I}{R_I^{2.5}}}{\sum \dfrac{1}{R_I^{2.5}}} \qquad (11.1)$$

The following code is the simplest implementation of this formula in two dimensions:

```
for(S=C=j=0;j<n;j++)
  {
  d=hypot(X[j]-x,Y[j]-y);
  if(d<DBL_EPSILON)
     d=DBL_EPSILON;
  d=pow(d,2.5);
  s+=1./d;
  c+=C[j]/d;
  }
c/=s;
```

It is necessary to limit the distance so as to not divide by zero. If you're that close, it doesn't matter what the other points are. Depending on how the known points are scattered, unwanted artifacts can arise. For example, if the known points are all clumped together on one side or corner of the domain, this will produce shadows, over-emphasizing the clumped data. These unwanted artifacts can often be eliminated by considering only the closest point in each of four quadrants (or eight octants).

A mistake often made when implementing a quadrant or octant search is to use the a=arctan2(y,x) function and then a series of if(a<M_PI/4.) statements. The arctan function takes far longer to execute than the multiplications, divisions, and even raising distance to a non-integral power. Do NOT use arctan for this purpose. A far easier and vastly faster process is:

```
for(i=0;i<4;i++)
  {
  iQ[i]=-1;
  Dq[i]=0.;
  }
for(i=0;i<n;i++)
  {
  dX=x-X[i];
```

```
        dY=y-Y[i];
        d=hypot(dX,dY);
        q=0;
        if(dX>0.)
          q|=1;
        if(dY>0.)
          q|=2;
        if(fabs(dX)>fabs(dY))
          q|=4;
        if(d<Dq[q])
          {
          Dq[q]=d;
          iQ[q]=i;
          }
        }
      for(C=s=q=0;q<8;q++)
        {
        if(iQ[q]>=0)
          {
          if(Dq[q]>DBL_EPSILON)
            d=pow(Dq[q],2.5);
          else
            d=DBL_EPSILON;
          S+=1./d
          C+=C[iQ[q]]/d;
          }
        }
      C/=s;
```

The three simple (and fast) comparisons (i.e., dX>0, dY>0, and |dX|>|dY|) uniquely determine the octant (0-7) by conditionally adding 3 bits (1, 2, and 4), which can only have values 0 through 7. Using the arctan takes at least eight times as long and provides no advantage whatsoever. The code above saves the (double) distance in Dq[8] and (integer) index in iQ[8]. The summation and application of pow(D,2.5) is applied as before. Of course, depending on where you are in the field, some of the octants may be empty, which is why we first fill the array iQ with minus ones.

Inverse distance code for 2D and 3D can be found in the online archive in folder examples in invdist.c Typical 2D results are shown in the following figure:

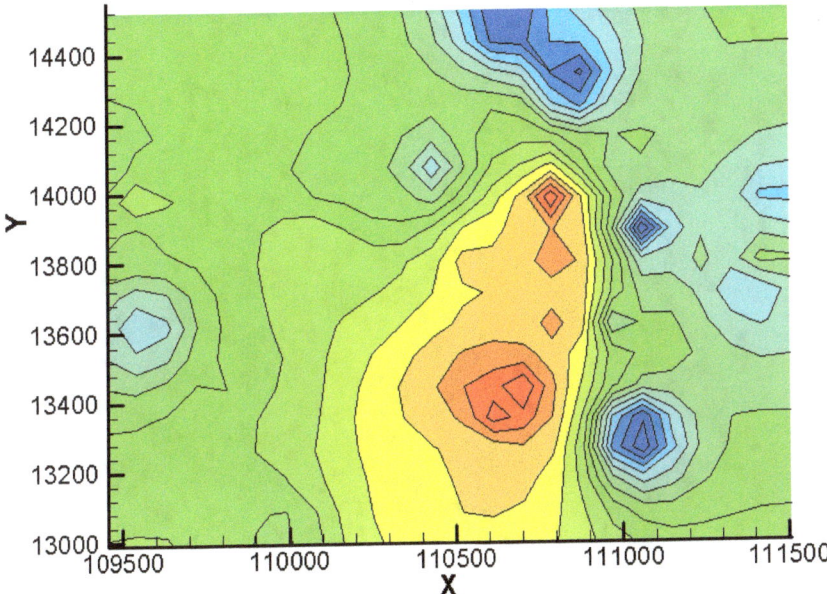

Figure 31. Typical Results of Inverse Distance Interpolation

Chapter 12. Kriging

Kriging is a form of Gaussian regression or interpolation used primarily in geostatistics. The original method was developed by Matheron[1] and based on the work of Krige.[2] There are actually a variety of formulas and techniques associated with the term *kriging*, making this designation rather ambiguous. Even a cursory search of the Internet will produce a dozen formulas, many of which (e.g., cos) bear no resemblance to the original concept of Gaussian approximation, which would exhibit an exponential departure outward from known points. Illustrations in one dimension show each data point blending into the next, but this is far removed from the two- and three-dimensional data to which this method is most often applied.

Tecplot™ is a very useful tool[3], which contains an implementation of this method that works well for some data but not for others. The same could be said for every other application I have used, so this is by no means a criticism of Tecplot™. T The implementation of kriging can be quite involved. It is not helpful that articles abound on the Web claiming to explain this process. Rarely do you find complete equations or code. If you compare the presentation on multiple sites you will find that they are not the same. I provide one implementation that I have found works well: kriging.c in the examples folder. The core code is:

```
for(w=0;w<64;w++)
  {
  for(d=0;d<Nd;d++)
    {
    C=Cd[d];
    for(c=0;c<Nd;c++)
      if(c-d)
        C-=Ck[d]*Bd[Nd*d+c];
    Ck[d]=fmax(Ck[d]/2.,fmin(2.*Cd[d],
      (w*Ck[d]+C)/(w+1)));
    }
  }
```

This code contains both 2D and 3D implementations, read data in from a file, and creates an output file containing the results distributed evenly over the domain at intervals you can specify or assign by default. There are several options that can be set in the code, including the linear expansion factor and

---

[1] Georges François Paul Marie Matheron (1930–2000) was French mathematician and civil engineer of mines, known as the founder of geostatistics and a co-founder (together with Jean Serra) of mathematical morphology.
[2] Danie Gerhardus Krige (1919–2013) South African statistician and mining engineer who pioneered the field of geostatistics and was professor at the University of the Witwatersrand.
[3] https://www.tecplot.com/

number of relaxations (iterations to smooth/spread the results). The same data set used for illustration in the previous chapter is shown below using kriging (with a lot of smoothing):

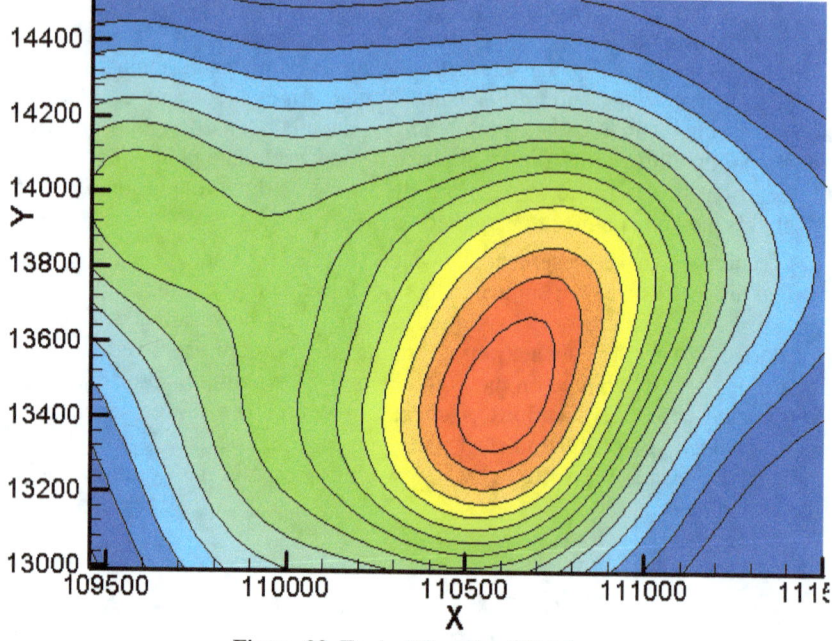

Figure 32. Typical Results of Kriging

Though not shown here, you could also apply several iterations of smoothening to the inverse distance results in the previous chapter. The corresponding code is included in the free archive.

Chapter 13. Simultaneous Linear Equations

The most effective way to solve simultaneous linear equations is Gauss-Jordan elimination with full column pivoting. Row pivoting is not optional, while column pivoting is; however, the additional effort often provides additional accuracy in the result. The basic problem is:

$$\begin{bmatrix} A_{11} & A_{12} & A_{13} \\ A_{21} & A_{22} & A_{23} \\ A_{31} & A_{32} & A_{33} \end{bmatrix} \times \begin{bmatrix} X_1 \\ X_2 \\ X_3 \end{bmatrix} = \begin{bmatrix} B_1 \\ B_2 \\ B_3 \end{bmatrix} \quad (13.1)$$

or

$$[A] \times [X] = [B] \quad (13.2)$$

Excel™ provides the functionality to perform such operations using LINEST (as described in Chapter 7), MMULT(), MINVERSE(), and several others. This operation is most effectively implemented in C or FORTRAN rather than VBA. A common example is curve-fitting, where the terms of matrix *A* are the individual points raised to sequentially-higher powers. This forms a matrix called a Vandermonde:

$$A = \begin{bmatrix} 1 & X_1 & X_1^2 & X_1^3 \\ 1 & X_2 & X_2^2 & X_2^3 \\ 1 & X_3 & X_3^2 & X_3^3 \\ 1 & X_n & X_n^2 & X_n^3 \end{bmatrix} \quad (13.3)$$

The reduction loop is quite simple:

```
for(i=k+1;i<n;i++)
   {
   a=A[n*i+k]/A[n*k+k];
   B[i]-=a*B[k];
   for(j=k+1;j<n;j++)
      A[n*i+j]-=a*A[n*k+j];
   }
```

Finding the pivot (largest element in the reduced matrix) is also simple:

```
for(j=k;j<n;j++)
   {
   a=fabs(A[n*i+j]);
   if(a>p)
      {
      ip=i;
      jp=j;
      p=a;
      }
```

}
Swapping the pivot into place is accomplished by:
```
if(ip!=k)
  {
  b=B[k];
  B[k]=B[ip];
  B[ip]=b;
  for(j=k;j<n;j++)
     {
     a=A[n*k+j];
     A[n*k+j]=A[n*ip+j];
     A[n*ip+j]=a;
     }
  }
if(jp!=k)
  {
  j=pivot[jp];
  pivot[jp]=pivot[k];
  pivot[k]=j;
  for(i=0;i<n;i++)
     {
     a=A[n*i+k];
     A[n*i+k]=A[n*i+jp];
     A[n*i+jp]=a;
     }
  }
```
Back-solving the matrix is accomplished by:
```
for(k=1;k<n;k++)
  {
  i=n-1-k;
  b=0.;
  for(j=i+1;j<n;j++)
    b+=A[n*i+j]*B[j];
  B[i]=(B[i]-b)/A[n*i+i];
  }
```
Finally, restoring the solution to the original order is accomplished by:
```
for(i=0;i<n;i++)
  B[pivot[i]]=A[i];
```
The code, along with an example, can be found in the online archive in the examples folder in matrix.c

Matrix Inversion

The Gauss-Jordan reduction algorithm can also be used to invert a matrix. For this we extend the matrix A by adding the identity matrix, I, off to the right. The identity matrix has all zeroes except for the diagonal elements, which are all one.

$$\begin{vmatrix} A_{11} & A_{12} & A_{13} \\ A_{21} & A_{22} & A_{23} \\ A_{31} & A_{32} & A_{33} \end{vmatrix} \begin{vmatrix} 1 & 0 & 0 \\ 0 & 1 & 0 \\ 0 & 0 & 1 \end{vmatrix} \qquad (13.4)$$

We first reduce the left side to an upper triangular matrix (all zeroes below the diagonal), then continue on backwards to make all the elements above the diagonal zero. When we're done, the left side (that was A) will be the identity matrix and the right side will be the inverse, A^{-1}. The back-solve (also using both row and column pivoting) goes from n-2 down to zero:

```
for(k=n-2;k>=0;k--)
  {
  i=ipivot[k];
  if(i!=k)
    {
    for(j=0;j<n;j++)
      {
      a=A[n*k+j];
      A[n*k+j]=-A[n*i+j];
      A[n*i+j]=a;
      }
    }
  j=jpivot[k];
  if(j!=k)
    {
    for(i=0;i<n;i++)
      {
      a=A[n*i+k];
      A[n*i+k]=-A[n*i+j];
      A[n*i+j]=a;
      }
    }
  }
```

The code is also in matrix.c.

Chapter 14. Linear Equations with Linear Constraints

Sometimes we want to add constraints to a problem. A common example of this would be a least-squares curve fit that matches exactly at one or more points. This would then be called linear least-squares with linear constraints. Because we cannot achieve the global minimum (in the least-squares sense) and *also* require exact agreement at one or more points, we must somehow *loosen up* the minimization requirement without making the problem nonlinear. This modified goal is accomplished with Lagrange multipliers. In this particular case, we don't care what the value of these terms (the Lagrange multipliers) are, but there are some problems for which these have significance. There are many articles on the Web regarding Lagrange multipliers.

The first part of our problem is represented by Equation 13.2. The exact match requirement is represented by:

$$[C][X]=[D] \qquad (14.1)$$

We combine Equations 13.2 and 14.1 to form the augmented matrix:

$$\begin{bmatrix} A & C^T \\ C & 0 \end{bmatrix}\begin{bmatrix} X \\ \Lambda \end{bmatrix}=\begin{bmatrix} B \\ D \end{bmatrix} \qquad (14.2)$$

Here C^T is the transpose of C and Λ is the column vector (matrix of dimension n×1) containing the Lagrange multipliers. If we expand this augmented matrix and examine each piece we could see that it does indeed satisfy both $AX+C^T\Lambda=B$ and $CX=D$. Remember, we can't satisfy both $AX=B$ and $CX=D$. In order to add $CX=D$ as a requirement, we have loosened up $AX=B$ by adding the term $C^T\Lambda$. The code for implementing this is also in matrix.c, as well as an illustration of its use. The function call is:

```
int LinearLeastSquaresWithLinearConstraints(double*A,
double*B, int m, double*C, double*D, int n, double*X)
```

where m is the number of linear equations and also the number of rows and columns in A and rows in B. The number of constraints is n, which is the rows in C and D. The number of columns in C must be the same as in A (that is, m). Our example is fitting a 4th order polynomial ($y=c_0+c_1x+c_2x^2+c_3x^3+c_4x^4$) to exp(x). We build the matrix A (which is actually A^TA) and B (which is actually A^TB) with the following code. We want an exact match at 2 of the 7 points selected and so we build C and D within the same loop for simplicity.

```
for(c=r=0;r<nr;r++)
{
x=r;
y=exp(x);
for(t=0;t<nt;t++)
   A[nt*r+t]=powi(x,t);
B[r]=y;
if(r%(nr/nc)==0&&c<nc)
```

```
        {
        for(t=0;t<nt;t++)
          C[nt*c+t]=A[nt*r+t];
        D[c]=B[r];
        c++;
        }
    }
```

We next create A^T (the transpose of A) and perform the two matrix multiplications:

```
    MatrixTranspose(A,At,nr,nt);
    MatrixMultiply(At,A,AtA,nt,nr,nt);
    MatrixMultiply(At,B,AtB,nt,nr,1);
```

The final step is calling:

```
    r=LinearEquationsWithLinearConstraints(
       AtA,AtB,nt,C,D,nc,X);
```

This function combines the matrices to form the augmented matrix and calls the Gauss-Jordan function to solve the resulting equations:

```
    for(i=0;i<m;i++)
      {
      for(j=0;j<m;j++)
        AC[l*i+j]=A[m*i+j];
      DL[i]=B[i];
      }
    for(i=0;i<n;i++)
      {
      for(j=0;j<m;j++)
        {
        AC[l*(m+i)+j  ]=
        AC[l*   j  +m+i]=C[m*i+j];
        }
      DL[m+i]=D[i];
      }
    i=MatrixSolve(AC,DL,1);
```

Chapter 15. Nonlinear Optimization in One Dimension

This is the process of finding the minimum or maximum of a function in one variable. The function is necessarily nonlinear, as linear functions (straight lines) don't exhibit a minimum or maximum. We build the algorithm to handle a minimum. If a maximum is sought, simply use the same algorithm on the inverse. The simplest effective algorithm for this is Brent's Method.[4] Articles on this approach are readily found on the Web and so we will not delve into the details here, only the implementation, which is illustrated in the following figure:

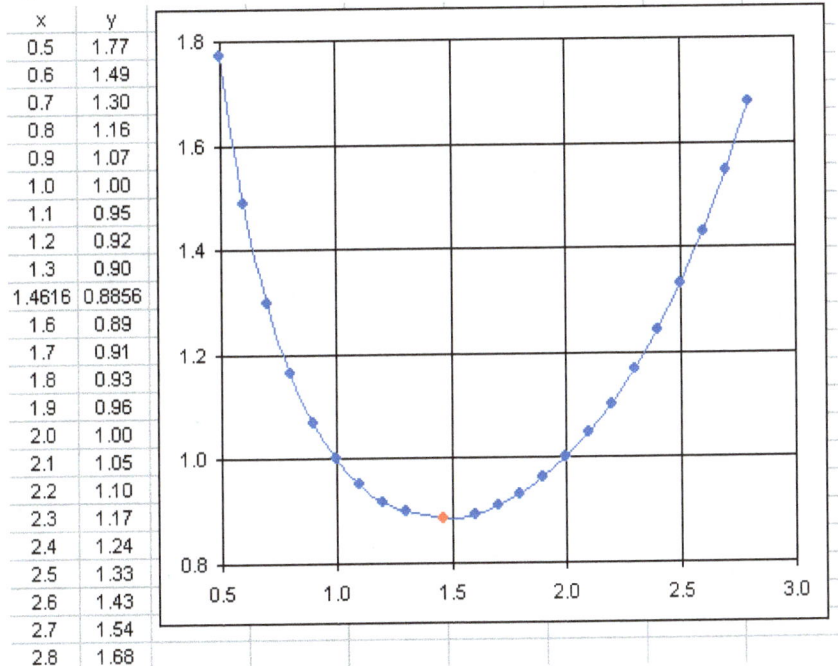

Figure 33. Illustration of Brent's Method

The algorithm is simple to implement:

```
double Brent(double x1,double x3,double func(double),
    int itmax,double eps,double*x2)
{
int iter;
double x,y1,y2,y3;
*x2=(x1+x3)/2.;
```

---

[4] Brent, R. P., *Algorithms for Minimization without Derivatives*, Chapter 4: An Algorithm with Guaranteed Convergence for Finding a Zero of a Function, Prentice-Hall, Englewood Cliffs, NJ, 1973.

```c
    y1=func(x1);
    y2=func(*x2);
    y3=func(x3);
    if(y2>=y1||y2>=y3)
       return(y2);
    for(iter=0;iter<itmax;iter++)
       {
       x=y1*(*x2-x3)+y2*(x3-x1)+(x1-*x2)*y3;
       if(fabs(x)<eps*(x3-*x2))
          break;
       x=((*x2*(*x2)-x3*x3)*y1+(x3*x3-x1*x1)*y2
          +(x1*x1-*x2*(*x2))*y3)/x/2.;
       if(x<*x2-eps)
          {
          x3=*x2;
          y3=y2;
          }
       else if(x>*x2+eps)
          {
          x1=*x2;
          y1=y2;
          }
       else
          break;
       *x2=x;
       y2=func(*x2);
       }
    return(y2);
    }
```

This example converges in 5 iterations requiring only 8 function calls. A spreadsheet (Brent.xls) containing the VBA implementation can be found in the examples folder. The C implementation (Brent.c) can also be found there.

Chapter 16. Nonlinear Optimization in Multiple Dimensions

While there are many algorithms for performing this task, most of these require the partial derivatives of the function being minimized or maximized, which is often not available analytically or tedious to compute. For this reason we use the derivative-free algorithm developed by Broyden.[5] This algorithm is based on Newton's method, in which can be expressed in one dimension, y(x), by the following:

$$x_{n+1} = x_n - \frac{y(x_n)}{\left(\frac{dy}{dx}\right)_{x_n}} \qquad (16.1)$$

where the next step (x_{n+1}) is equal to the current step (x_n) plus the value of the function at the current position divided by the derivative at that point. As we are seeking a minimum or maximum, what we really want is the point where the partial derivative of the function is zero, so that our current value is the partial derivative and the denominator in Equation 16.1 becomes the second partial derivative. We might express this condition in matrix form:

$$[x_{i,n+1}] = [x_{i,n}] - \frac{\left[\frac{\partial y}{\partial x_i}\right]}{\left[\frac{\partial^2 y}{\partial x_i \partial x_j}\right]} \qquad (16.2)$$

The numerator contains the first partial derivatives and is called the gradient. The denominator contains the second partial derivatives and is called the Hessian. This looks simple enough but rarely works well, as the Hessian is often problematic to compute and the matrix often becomes singular (i.e., divide by zero). Broyden's method begins with an estimate of the Hessian (pick several random points) and proceeds one step at a time, updating the Hessian each time, but only in the direction of the previous step because that's the only additional information we have about its behavior. This is called a rank-one update. A full (non-singular) $n \times n$ matrix has rank n. A single vector (i.e., row or column) that spans only one dimension of this n-space has rank 1. We a single step (x_{n+1}-x_n) by the formula:

$$[s_n] = [x_{n+1}] - [x_n] \qquad (16.3)$$

Rearranging Equation 16.2 and multiplying through by the denominator yields:

---

[5] Broyden, C., "A New Method of Solving Nonlinear Simultaneous Equations," *Computational Journal*, Vol. 12, pp. 94-99, 1969.

$$[H_n][s_n] = -[g_n] \quad (16.4)$$

that is, the Hessian times the step is equal to minus the gradient. The rank-one update can be expressed by:

$$H_{n+1} = H_n + \frac{(g_n - H_n s_n)s_n^T}{s_n^T s_n} \quad (16.5)$$

Broyden's method has been used to solve a wide variety of such problems and many articles have been published on the subject.[6] Locating the minimum (or maximum) of a function in two dimensions is like finding the lowest (or highest) point on a topography map, which is illustrated in this next figure:

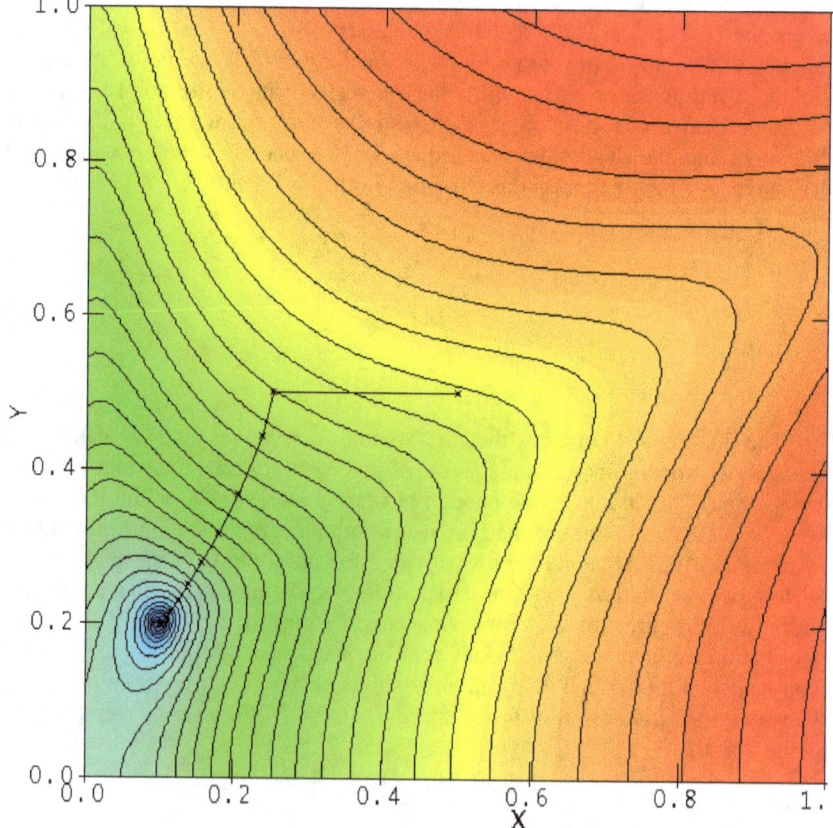

Figure 34. Example of Broyden's Method in 2D

---

[6] Benton, D. J., "Applications of a Hybrid Derivative-Free Algorithm for Locating Extrema," Society of Industrial and Applied Mathematics (SIAM), Southeastern Regional Seminar, Cullowhee, North Carolina, April 12-13, 1991.

The lowest point is in blue ant the highest in red. The black line represents the solution path, which steps from point-to-point until it reaches the center of the bluest contour. The code can be found in the examples folder in Broyden.c, which includes 8 complete examples. My suggestion is to find the one most like your problem and adapt it as needed. The call is simple:

```
int Broyden(void func(double*,double*),double*Xmin,
double*Xmax,double*X,int n,int m,int maxcalls)
```

You supply the function, which must accept n variables and return m residuals (or errors). Also $n \leq m$. *Xmin* and *Xmax* are arrays containing the n minimum and maximum values of the independent variable, *X* (see examples within the code). Use *maxcalls* to limit the number of steps (or attempts to find the minimum). A typical residual function is listed below:

```
void resid3(double*X,double*F)
   {
   F[0]=75.*X[0]*X[0]-169.*X[1]*X[1]/9.;
   F[1]=845.*X[0]*X[1]*X[1]/3.-125.*X[0]*X[0]*X[0]-1.;
   }
```

which receives two values (*X[0]* and *X[1]*) and returns two (*F[0]* and *F[1]*). Typical values of *Xmin* and *Xmax* are listed below:

```
      double Xmin[2]={-2.,-2.};
      double Xmax[2]={ 2., 2.};
```

Chapter 17. Fast Fourier Transform and Beyond

Surprisingly, many articles about the Fast Fourier Transform (FFT) on the Web skip right over the most astonishing part: where the transcendental values come from. Perhaps fast floating point processors have been available for so long that these authors have forgotten how many steps it take to calculate a sine or cosine and the time required. Sines and cosines form an orthogonal set over the interval -π to +π (or 0 to 2π); therefore, we can take advantage of this property.

In order to determine the coefficients for our approximation, we will need to calculate a series of sums. This means we must calculate a whole bunch of sines and cosines. While such may now be possible in microseconds, it hasn't always been this way, which is why FFTs are so useful. Consider the following trigonometric identities:

$$\sin(a+b) = \sin(a)\cos(b) + \cos(a)\sin(b)$$
$$\cos(a+b) = \cos(a)\cos(b) - \sin(a)\sin(b)$$
(17.1)

The sums we will be calculating include sin(x), sin(2x), sin(3x), etc. and cos(x), cos(2x), cos(3x), etc. Sin(2x) is equal to sin(x+x) and sin(3x) is equal to sin(2x+x), etc. We need only calculate sin(x) and cos(x), because all the higher order terms come from repeated applications of Equation 17.1. This is the *magic of the FFT!* The code to implement this is almost trivial. The following snippets illustrate the Slow and Fast Fourier Transform. Note that the transcendental functions (i.e., sin and cos) are inside the inner loop in the former and outside in the latter.

```
void SlowFourierTransform(double*f,int n,double*c,double*s,int m)
  {
  int i,j;
  double ci,cj,cs,si,sj,ss;
  for(i=0;i<m;i++)
    {
    for(cj=cs=sj=ss=j=0;j<n;j++)
      {
      ci=cos(2*i*(j+1)*M_PI/n);
      si=sin(2*i*(j+1)*M_PI/n);
      cj+=f[j]*ci;
      sj+=f[j]*si;
      cs+=ci*ci;
      ss+=si*si;
      }
    c[i]=cj/cs;
    if(i)
      s[i]=sj/ss;
    }
  }
```

```
void FastFourierTransform(double*f,int
n,double*c,double*s,int m)
  {
  int i,j;
  double cc,ci,cj,ck,si,sj,sk,ss;
  for(i=0;i<m;i++)
    {
    ci=cj=cos(2*i*M_PI/n);
    si=sj=sin(2*i*M_PI/n);
    for(c[i]=s[i]=cc=ss=j=0;j<n;j++)
      {
      c[i]+=cj*f[j];
      s[i]+=sj*f[j];
      cc+=cj*cj;
      ss+=sj*sj;
      ck=ci*cj-si*sj;
      sk=si*cj+ci*sj;
      cj=ck;
      sj=sk;
      }
    c[i]/=cc;
    if(i)
      s[i]/=ss;
    }
  }
```

If $f(x)$ is a periodic function over the interval $-\pi$ to $+\pi$, the Fourier series is defined by:

$$F(x) = \frac{a_0}{2} + \sum_{n=1}^{\infty} a_n \cos(nx) + b_n \sin(nx) \qquad (17.2)$$

where the coefficients a_n and b_n are defined by:

$$a_n = \frac{1}{\pi} \int_{-\pi}^{\pi} f(x)\cos(nx)dx$$
$$b_n = \frac{1}{\pi} \int_{-\pi}^{\pi} f(x)\sin(nx)dx \qquad (17.3)$$

We will consider three simple examples (step, saw tooth, and ramp) for which the analytical solutions are readily available to illustrate this process and validate the calculations. These are illustrated in the following figure:

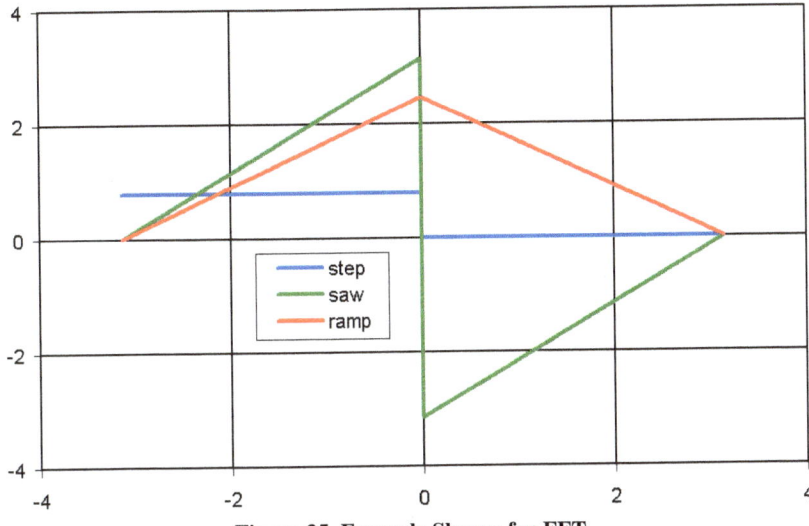

Figure 35. Example Shapes for FFT

The step series is given by: $a_n=0$, $b_n=1/n$, $n=1,3,5,...$ The preceding C function yields: 0, 1, 0, 0.33332, 0.00001, 0.19998, 0.00001, 0.14284, 0.00002, 0.11108. The saw tooth is given by $a_n=0$, $b_n=((-1)^{n+1})/n$, $n=1, 2, 3, ...$ The preceding C function yields: 0, 0.99902, -0.49999, 0.33299, -0.24998, 0.19978, -0.16663, 0.14268, -0.12496, 0.11095. The ramp is given by: $a_0=b_n=0$, $a_n=1/n^2$, $n=1, 3, 5, ...$ The preceding C function yields: 0.00181, 1.00121, 0.0012, 0.11232, 0.0012, 0.04121, 0.0012, 0.02161, 0.0012, 0.01355. Output of the code follows, including a comparison of results and processor time:

```
                Square Wave
        <-----slow----->  <-----fast----->
   i     c[i]     s[i]      c[i]     s[i]
   0   0.00016  0.00000   0.00016  0.00000
   1  -0.00094  1.00000  -0.00094  1.00000
   2   0.00031  0.00000   0.00031  0.00000
   3  -0.00094  0.33333  -0.00094  0.33333
   4   0.00031  0.00000   0.00031  0.00000
   5  -0.00094  0.20000  -0.00094  0.20000
   6   0.00031  0.00000   0.00031  0.00000
   7  -0.00094  0.14285  -0.00094  0.14285
   8   0.00031  0.00000   0.00031  0.00000
   9  -0.00094  0.11111  -0.00094  0.11111
       0.05480  seconds   0.00448  seconds
                 Saw Tooth
        <-----slow----->  <-----fast----->
   i     c[i]     s[i]      c[i]     s[i]
   0   0.00031  0.00000   0.00031  0.00000
   1  -0.00126  0.99960  -0.00126  0.99960
```

```
2   0.00126  -0.50000   0.00126  -0.50000
3  -0.00126   0.33320  -0.00126   0.33320
4   0.00126  -0.25000   0.00126  -0.25000
5  -0.00126   0.19992  -0.00126   0.19992
6   0.00126  -0.16666   0.00126  -0.16666
7  -0.00126   0.14279  -0.00126   0.14279
8   0.00126  -0.12499   0.00126  -0.12499
9  -0.00126   0.11106  -0.00126   0.11106
    0.05460  seconds    0.00446  seconds
                    Ramp
    <-----slow----->   <-----fast----->
i     c[i]      s[i]     c[i]      s[i]
0   0.00049   0.00000   0.00049   0.00000
1   1.00000   0.00063   1.00000   0.00063
2  -0.00000  -0.00000  -0.00000  -0.00000
3   0.11111   0.00021   0.11111   0.00021
4  -0.00000  -0.00000  -0.00000  -0.00000
5   0.04000   0.00013   0.04000   0.00013
6  -0.00000  -0.00000  -0.00000  -0.00000
7   0.02041   0.00009   0.02041   0.00009
8  -0.00000  -0.00000  -0.00000  -0.00000
9   0.01235   0.00007   0.01235   0.00007
    0.05328  seconds    0.00446  seconds
```

The C code (for both slow and fast Fourier transform) may be found in the online archive in the examples folder in fft.c along with an Excel™ spreadsheet also illustrating the calculations, fft.xls. The C code also contains a speed test and example of calling the microsecond timer so that the two (slow and fast) algorithms may be compared for their efficiency.

Perhaps the most fascinating application of the FFT is medical imaging, including CAT[7] or MRI scans. A beam is passed through the patient, producing a time-varying analog signal. The signal is reduced to frequency components on arrival by performing an FFT. This also digitizes the signal—all digitally with modern computers, but early implementations used a mixture of analog and digital strategies to accomplish essentially the same result. The sensor is rotated slightly and another beam is passed through the patient. This sensor positioning naturally produces data in polar coordinates, rather than rectangular (i.e., Cartesian). This is called the Radon Transform after Austrian mathematician Johann Karl August Radon (1887-1956).

---

[7] The acronym CAT stands for Computer Aided Tomography and often refers to a rotating X-ray scanner. Magnetic Resonance Imaging is actually a type of CAT scan, although it uses a powerful magnetic field instead of X-rays to sample the patient. A Positron Emission Tomography (PET) scanner is yet another type of Computer Aided Tomography, which uses particles instead of X-rays or magnetic fields.

Beyond the FFT

The FFT is useful and efficient because the sine and cosine are orthogonal, making application much less complicated (and stable) then progressively larger matrix solutions, as one might use with simple polynomial approximation. There are many other orthogonal functions, which can be utilized in a similar manner. For some types of data, these other functions are a better choice than sine and cosine. The seven most commonly used orthogonal polynomials, the intervals, and corresponding weighting functions are listed in the following table:

Table 17.1 Most Common Orthogonal Polynomials

name	interval	w(x)
Fourier (sin, cos)	$-\pi$ to π	1
Legendre	-1 to 1	1
Jacobi	-1 to 1	$(1-x)^a(1+x)^b$
Gebenbauer (ultraspherical)	-1 to 1	$(1-x^2)^{a-\frac{1}{2}}$
Chebyshev (1st kind)	-1 to 1	$(1-x)^{-\frac{1}{2}}$
Chebyshev (2nd kind)	-1 to 1	$(1-x)^{\frac{1}{2}}$
Laguerre	0 to ∞	$e^{-x}x^a$
Hermite	$-\infty$ to ∞	e^{-x^2}

Sin and cos aren't polynomials, but are included in the table to illustrate two things: the interval and the weighting function. The orthogonality condition is:

$$\int_a^b P_i(x)P_j(x)w(x)dx = \begin{cases} \neq 0 \text{ if } i = j \\ = 0 \text{ if } i \neq j \end{cases} \quad (17.4)$$

The interval is different for the Fourier series and the Legendre polynomials, but these are the only ones with no weighting function (i.e., $w(x)=1$). All the others have a weighting function that varies over the interval. The Laguerre and Hermite are the only ones with infinite intervals, the former semi-infinite and the latter fully infinite. The rest operate over a finite domain. Which ones to use is determined by the domain and the weighting function. Select the ones that correspond to your problem. More details about these and other functions may be found in Chapter 22 (especially sections 22.18-22.20) of the seminal reference for applied mathematicians, Abramowitz and Stegun.[8] Choose the functions that fit the domain of your data, also considering the weighting function. All of the following examples, code, and data can be found in the online archive accompanying *Orthogonal Functions*, located on the same Web page at the link below the Preface of this text.

---

[8] Abramowitz, M. and I. A. Stegun, *Handbook of Mathematical Functions* first published by the National Bureau of Standards as Technical Monograph No. 55. This invaluable reference may be obtained free online as a PDF from several different web sites.

Legendre Polynomials

For our first example we will consider a data set approximated by Legendre polynomials, which are shown in Figure 3 on page iv. The approximations are shown in this next figure:

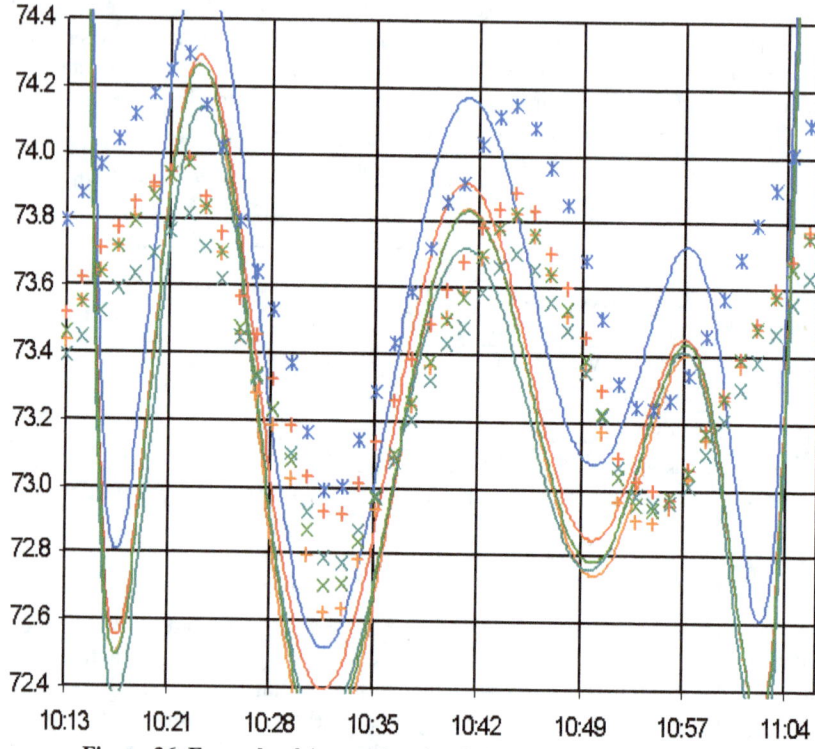

Figure 36. Example of Approximation Using Legendre Polynomials

This function calculates the Legendre polynomials:
```
double Legendre(int n,double x)
  {
  int i;
  double l1,l2,l3;
  if(n<0)
    return(0.);
  if(n<1)
    return(1.);
  if(n<2)
    return(x);
  l2=1.;
  l3=x;
  for(i=2;i<=n;i++)
    {
```

```
    l1=l2;
    l2=l3;
    l3=2.*x*l2-l1-(x*l2-l1)/i;
    }
 return(l3);
 }
```

Jacobi Polynomials

The Jacobi polynomials look like this:

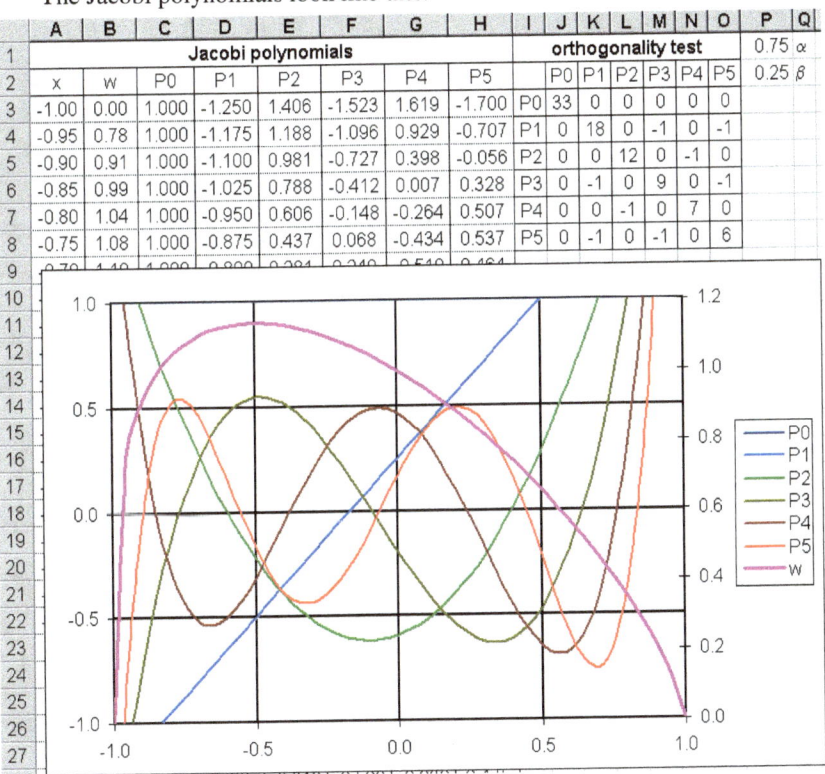

	A	B	C	D	E	F	G	H	I	J	K	L	M	N	O	P	Q
1				Jacobi polynomials							orthogonality test					0.75	α
2	x	w	P0	P1	P2	P3	P4	P5		P0	P1	P2	P3	P4	P5	0.25	β
3	-1.00	0.00	1.000	-1.250	1.406	-1.523	1.619	-1.700	P0	33	0	0	0	0	0		
4	-0.95	0.78	1.000	-1.175	1.188	-1.096	0.929	-0.707	P1	0	18	0	-1	0	-1		
5	-0.90	0.91	1.000	-1.100	0.981	-0.727	0.398	-0.056	P2	0	0	12	0	-1	0		
6	-0.85	0.99	1.000	-1.025	0.788	-0.412	0.007	0.328	P3	0	-1	0	9	0	-1		
7	-0.80	1.04	1.000	-0.950	0.606	-0.148	-0.264	0.507	P4	0	0	-1	0	7	0		
8	-0.75	1.08	1.000	-0.875	0.437	0.068	-0.434	0.537	P5	0	-1	0	-1	0	6		

Figure 37. Jacobi Polynomials

This function returns the Jacobi polynomials:

```
double Jacobi(int n,double alpha,double beta,double x)
 {
 int i;
 double c1,c2,c3,c4,p1,p2,p3;
 if(n<0)
   return(0.);
 p2=1.;
 if(n<1)
   return(p2);
```

```
    p3=(1.+0.5*(alpha+beta))*x+0.5*(alpha-beta);
    if(n<2)
       return(p3);
    for(i=2;i<=n;i++)
       {
       c1=2*i*(i+alpha+beta)*(2*i-2+alpha+beta);
       c2=(2*i-1+alpha+beta)*(2*i+alpha+beta)*(2*i-2+alpha+beta);
       c3=(2*i-1+alpha+beta)*(alpha+beta)*(alpha-beta);
       c4=-2*(i-1+alpha)*(i-1+beta)*(2*i+alpha+beta);
       p1=p2;
       p2=p3;
       p3=((c3+c2*x)*p2+c4*p1)/c1;
       }
    return(p3);
    }
```

Chebyshev Polynomials

The Chebyshev polynomials of the 1st kind are shown in Figure 4 on page iv. The following two functions return the 1st and 2nd Chebyshev polynomials:

```
double Cheby1(int n,double x)
   {
   int i;
   double T1,T2,T3;
   if(n<0)
      return(0.);
   if(n<1)
      return(1.);
   if(n<2)
      return(x);
   T2=1.;
   T3=x;
   for(i=2;i<=n;i++)
      {
      T1=T2;
      T2=T3;
      T3=2.*x*T2-T1;
      }
   return(T3);
   }
double Cheby2(int n,double x)
   {
   int i;
   double U1,U2,U3;
   if(n<0)
      return(0.);
   if(n<1)
      return(1.);
   if(n<2)
```

```
  return(2.*x);
U2=1.;
U3=2.*x;
for(i=2;i<=n;i++)
   {
   U1=U2;
   U2=U3;
   U3=2.*x*U2-U1;
   }
return(U3);
}
```

An example of Chebyshev approximation is shown in this next figure:

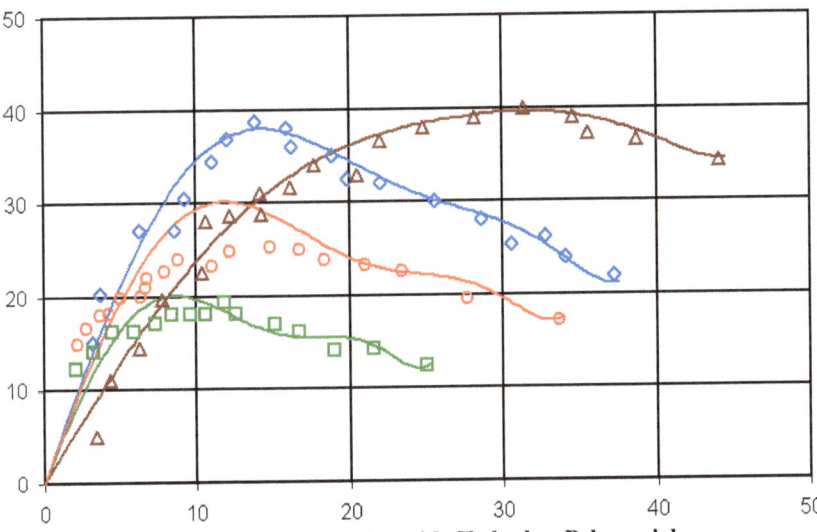

Figure 38. Approximation with Chebyshev Polynomials

This particular data set was the subject of much controversy with various interested parties arguing about every attempt to fit curves through the points (for example polynomials), as even small changes could mean vast sums in remediation or construction costs. The group finally agreed on the Chebyshev approximation as not biasing the outcome for or against any one of the parties.

Laguerre Polynomials

Laguerre polynomials are useful when the domain extends from zero to infinity, particularly in spherical and cylindrical geometries. The weighting function is $e^{-x}x^a$ so that the data will vanish at infinity plus you have some control over how fast by adjusting the parameter a to best meet the expectation. You can also optimize both the length scale (non-dimensionalizing x or the radius). The following function returns the Laguerre polynomials:

```
double Laguerre(int n,double x)
  {
  int i;
  double l1,l2,l3;
  if(n<0)
    return(0.);
  if(n<1)
    return(1.);
  l2=1.;
  l3=1.-x;
  for(i=2;i<=n;i++)
    {
    l1=l2;
    l2=l3;
    l3=((2*i-1-x)*l2-(i+1)*l1)/i;
    }
  return(l3);
  }
```

These are shown in the figure below:

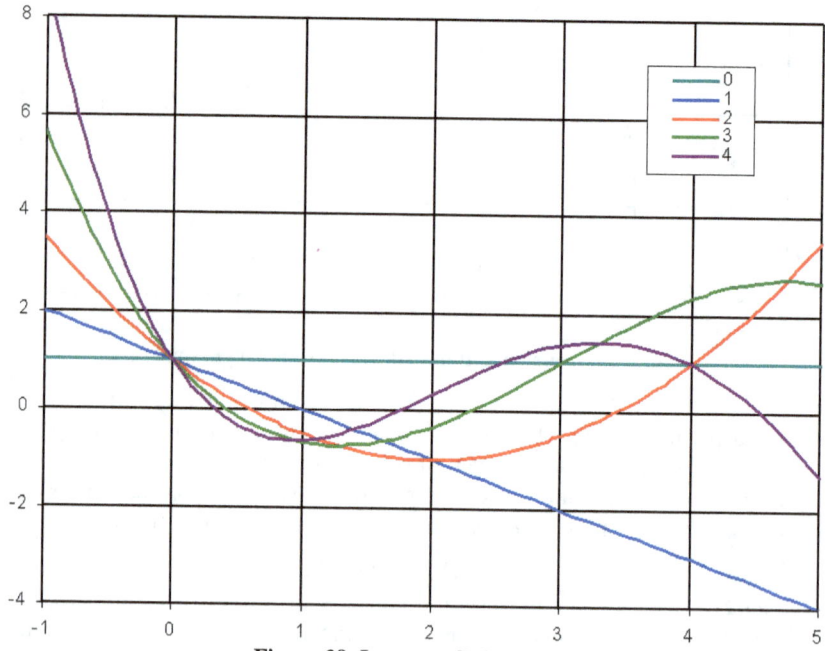

Figure 39. Laguerre Polynomials

Hermite Polynomials

Hermite polynomials extend from $-\infty$ to $+\infty$ and have a weighting function of e^{-x^2}, making them ideal for several types of data, including contaminants in air and surface or ground water. The integral over the domain is easily calculated so that the total mass is readily available and, if known, can be used to optimize the approximation. The Hermite polynomials are shown in this next figure:

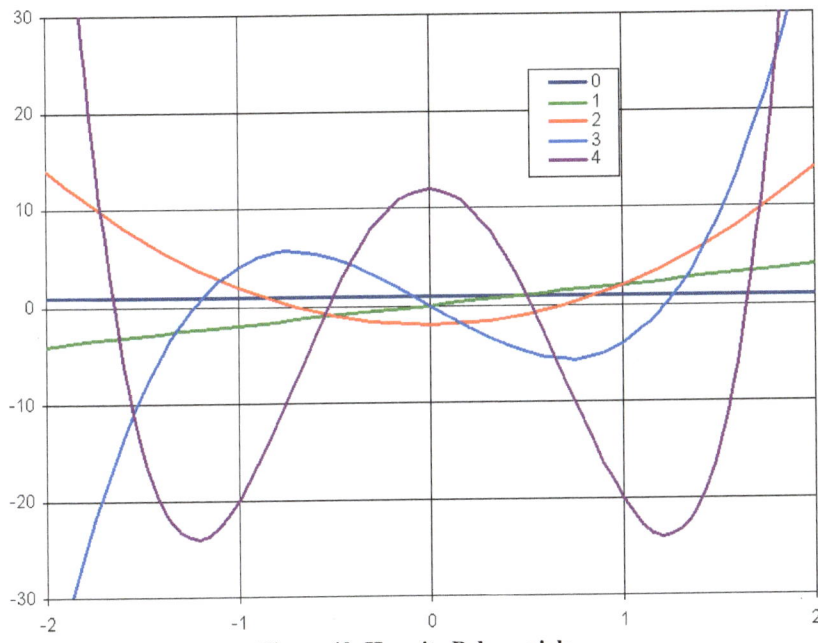

Figure 40. Hermite Polynomials

This function returns the Hermite polynomials:

```
double Hermite(int n,double x)
   {
   int i;
   double h1,h2,h3;
   if(n<0)
     return(0.);
   if(n<1)
     return(1.);
   h2=1.;
   h3=2.*x;
   for(i=2;i<=n;i++)
      {
      h1=h2;
      h2=h3;
      h3=2.*(x*h2-(i-1)*h1);
      }
   return(h3);
   }
```

Two codes (plume2d.c and plume3d.c) can be found in the online archive accompanying *Orthogonal Functions* in the examples\Hermite folder that will perform the necessary calculations required to arrive at an approximation of 2D or 3D data, respectively, creating output files (a surface or volume) along with the necessary files to plot the result. The core section of code that performs the orthogonalization is listed below:

```
for (m=0;m<mx*my;m++)
  {
  for (R=S=n=i=0;i<plume.polys;i++)
    {
    for (p=0;p<plume.poly[i].points;p++)
      {
      X=-extent+2.*extent*(plume.poly[i].east[p]
        -Xm)/(Xx-Xm);
      Y=-extent+2.*extent*(plume.poly[i].north[p]
        -Ym)/(Yx-Ym);
      Z=E[n++];
      P=Hermite(m/mx,Y)*Hermite(m%mx,X);
      W=exp(-(X*X+Y*Y)/2.);
      R+=Z*P*W;
      S+=P*P*W*W;
      }
    }
  C[m]=R/S;
  for (n=i=0;i<plume.polys;i++)
    {
    for (p=0;p<plume.poly[i].points;p++)
      {
      X=-extent+2.*extent*(plume.poly[i].east[p]
        -Xm)/(Xx-Xm);
      Y=-extent+2.*extent*(plume.poly[i].north[p]
        -Ym)/(Yx-Ym);
      W=exp(-(X*X+Y*Y)/2.);
      E[n++]-=C[m]*W*Hermite(m/mx,Y)*Hermite(m%mx,X);
      }
    }
  }
```

Hermite polynomials satisfy the following orthogonality condition:

$$\int_{-\infty}^{+\infty} Hn(x)Hm(x)e^{-x^2}dx = \begin{cases} \sqrt{\pi}2^n n! & if\ (n=m) \\ 0 & if\ (n \neq m) \end{cases} \quad (17.5)$$

The coefficients for the approximation are calculated using:

$$Cn = \frac{\int_{-\infty}^{+\infty} F(x)Hn(x)e^{-x^2}dx}{\int_{-\infty}^{+\infty} H_n^2(x)e^{-x^2}dx} \quad (17.6)$$

The following figure shows two contaminant plumes approximated using Hermite polynomials:

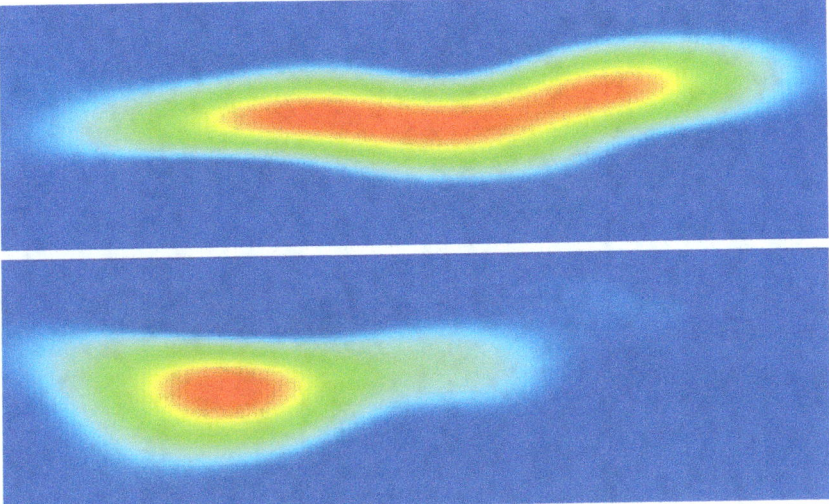

Figure 41. Approximated Contaminant Plumes

Chapter 18. Random Numbers

Occasionally you need random numbers, like when creating a Monte Carlo simulation. There are two basic types of random numbers: 1) uniformly-distributed; and 2) normally-distributed. These are illustrated in the following figure:

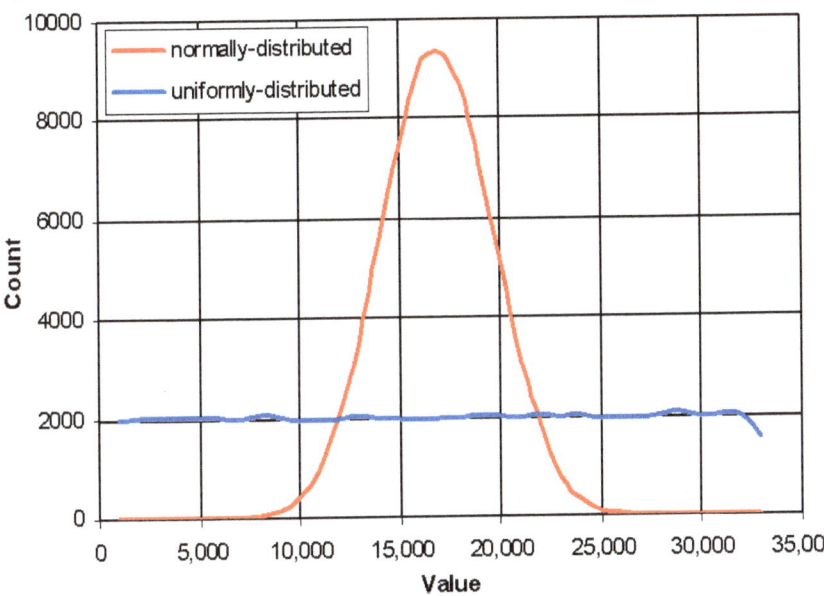

Figure 42. 65,534 Random Integers

The tail on the right side of the blue line is a defect in the algorithm used to create the numbers. These may be found in the examples folder in random.xls. In this spreadsheet you will find integers, reals, and more on what *normal* means. Excel™ provides a function: =rand() in the spreadsheet and =Rnd() in VBA code. These return the same thing, a uniformly-distributed real number between zero and one. The rand() function in C returns uniformly-distributed random integers between 0 and 32767, that is 15-bit unsigned integers. These are only approximately distributed uniformly, but in most cases this is adequate. The algorithm used to generate these numbers in the ANSI standard library is:

```
static unsigned long int next=1;
short int rand(void)
  {
  next=next*1103515245UL+12345UL;
  return((unsigned short int)(next/0x10000UL)&0x7FFF);
  }
```

This algorithm relies on repetitive multiplication resulting in an overflow condition each time and is typical. The algorithm used by Excel is quite similar, except that the integers are converted to reals. The sequence of random numbers always starts at the same place unless it is *seeded*. The two seeding functions in the standard library are:

```
void srand(unsigned short int seed)
  {
  next=seed;
  }
void randomize(void)
  {
  next=(unsigned long)time(NULL);
  }
```

These standard functions only span 15 bits. Should you require larger random numbers or more variety, several functions are available. A simple way of generating 32-bit random integers is listed here:

```
DWORD drand()
  {
  union{DWORD d;BYTE b[4];}u;
  u.b[0]=(BYTE)(rand()&0xFF);
  u.b[1]=(BYTE)(rand()&0xFF);
  u.b[2]=(BYTE)(rand()&0xFF);
  u.b[3]=(BYTE)(rand()&0x7F);
  return(u.d);
  }
```

These are uniformly-distributed random numbers, that is, random numbers that have a flat probability distribution, as illustrated in the preceding figure. What we most often need is normally-distributed random numbers that have a bell-shaped probability distribution. The simplest way to produce normally distributed integers from uniformly-distributed ones is the following formula:

```
int nrand()
  {
  int i,r;
  for(r=i=0;i<12;i++)
    r+=rand();
  return(r/12);
  }
```

A slight modification of this formula can be used to create normally-distributed real numbers having a mean of 0 and a standard deviation of 1:

```
double randnorm()
  {
  int i;
  double r;
  for(r=i=0;i<12;i++)
    r+=rand()/32767.;
  return((r-6.)/6.);
  }
```

The real/integer adjustment is the reverse when working with VBA. The function above can be used to create normally-distributed numbers having a mean of *a* and s standard deviation of *s*:

```
double randist(double a,double s)
  {
  return(a+6.*s*randnorm());
  }
```

All of the code listed above can be found in random.c along with an algorithm for shuffling cards, an example of which is:

```
4S  3C  7C  KC  QH  9C  3S  10C  4D  7H   JS   4C  KS
9S  2H  2S  6H  5D  8C  KH  6S   2D  10S  QC   AS  3H
AD  7S  QS  QD  4H  7D  3D  JC   8D  JD   10D  9H  KD
AC  2C  AH  5C  9D  6C  8H  8S   JH  5S   10H  6D  5H
```

You can find many illustrations of using random numbers in my book, *Monte Carlo Simulation*. One example is battling monsters and their chances of winning:

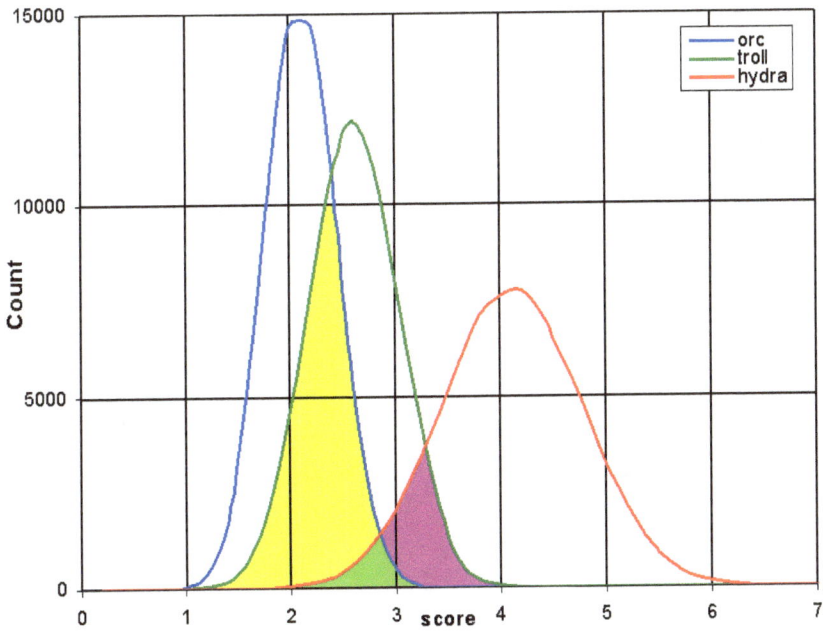

Figure 43. Battling Monsters' Chances of Winning

Chapter 19. Predicting a Trend or Storm

Perhaps the most familiar trend at the present is the COVID-19 pandemic that has occupied much of the news over the past two years. Data are readily available from a variety of sources. For this example we use daily numbers from the CDC from 1/6/2020 through 3/10/2020. We have an expectation: the number of cases (or deaths) will roughly follow a bell-shaped curve or *wave*, rising early in the cycle, peaking, and falling off. We have the daily rates and also the cumulative running total in a spreadsheet, COVID.xls. Excel™ provides a function for the normal distribution: =NORMDIST(x, mean, standard deviation, cumulative), where x is the current value (the date), *mean* is the date of the peak, *standard deviation* is a measure of the width of the peak, and *cumulative* is a logical switch that we set to FALSE for this problem. We don't know the mean, standard deviation, or the height of the peak. We use Solver to obtain the best fit for each day after accumulating 30 days of data. The spreadsheet looks like this:

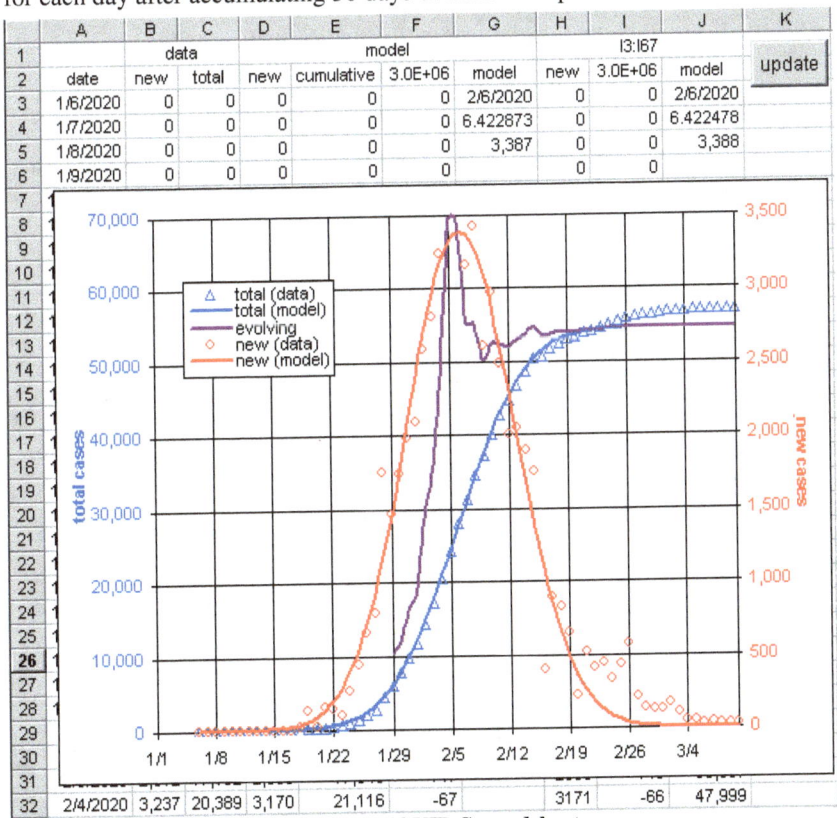

Figure 44. COVID Spreadsheet

The red circles represent the daily data (refer to the scale on the right). The blue triangles are the cumulative deaths (refer to the scale on the left). The red curve is the bell-shaped curve that best fits the data (both the red circles and blue triangles, as these are linked). The purple wavy curve is the predicted total number of deaths for this wave, which evolves over time, as we accumulate more data. The Solver is used for each day past 2/6/2020, so we put this inside a macro, which is activated by pushing the button. The code is listed below:

```
Option Explicit
Private Sub CommandButton1_Click()
  Dim i As Integer, s As String
  For i = 26 To 67
    s = Str(i)
    s = Mid(s, 2, Len(s) - 1)
    s = "I3:I" & s
    Range("H1").Value = s
    SolverOk SetCell:="$I$2", MaxMinVal:=2, ValueOf:="0", ByChange:="$J$3:$J$5"
    SolverSolve UserFinish:=True
    Cells(i, 10).Value = Range("J5").Value * Range("J4").Value * Sqr(2 * 3.1415926)
  Next i
End Sub
```

We see in this figure that after only 30 days of data, we predict 10,442 deaths. The highest predicted deaths is 69,650. The final predicted number of deaths 54,541 and actual deaths as of 3/10/2020 was 57,051. While this is an interesting numerical example, sadly this was only the first of several waves, many more people died, and it may not be over yet.

Normally-Distributed Probability of Occurrence

Most processes are accompanied by some expectation, whether a shape of the curve or repetitive cycle. Natural events, such as storms, tidal waves and surges, earthquakes, and volcanoes often exhibit similar behavior as to their frequency. The COVID illustration graph shows an important relationship for events that exhibit a normal distribution: the red bell-shaped curve accumulates (adds up to) the blue S-shaped one. If we can assume storms follow this shape (i.e., few at the low end, rising to a peak of frequency at some average, and falling off to ever fewer occurrences at the high end), we can use this curve to predict the outliers based on the past. That is, we can estimate the storm that might occur once in 100 years (i.e., the 100-year storm).

Scientist have been making these estimates long before Excel™ so how did they do it? To facilitate this process, we first define two terms: µ the average and σ the standard deviation. The red probability distribution curve (see Excel help) is given by:

$$dp = \frac{e^{-\frac{(x-\mu)^2}{2\sigma^2}}}{\sqrt{2\pi}\sigma} \qquad (19.1)$$

The blue cumulative probability, *p*, is the integral of the distribution, which becomes the Gauss error function, *erf( )*:

$$p = \int_{-\infty}^{z} \frac{e^{-\frac{z^2}{2}}}{\sqrt{2\pi}} dz = \frac{1}{2}\left[1 + erf\left(\frac{z}{\sqrt{2}}\right)\right] \quad (19.2)$$

where:

$$z = \frac{x - \mu}{\sigma} \quad (19.3)$$

Example: IQ Scores

The variable *z* is our transform dimensionless coordinate, as x, μ, and σ all have the same units (e.g., date or time in the case of COVID data). If we plot the blue cumulative probability curve (using TRUE in the Excel call) vs. the transform coordinate, z, the S-shaped curve becomes a straight line. We illustrate this with the familiar case of IQ scores. Consider the following fabricated list of 36,721 IQ scores (see IQ.xls in examples folder):

	A	B	C	D	E	F	G	H	I	J
1	IQ Scores			cumulative	Z					
2	score	46	number	probability	score					
3	80	47	2	0.0000545	-3.56					
4	123	48	0	0.0000545	-3.49					
5	104	49	4	0.0001634	-3.42					

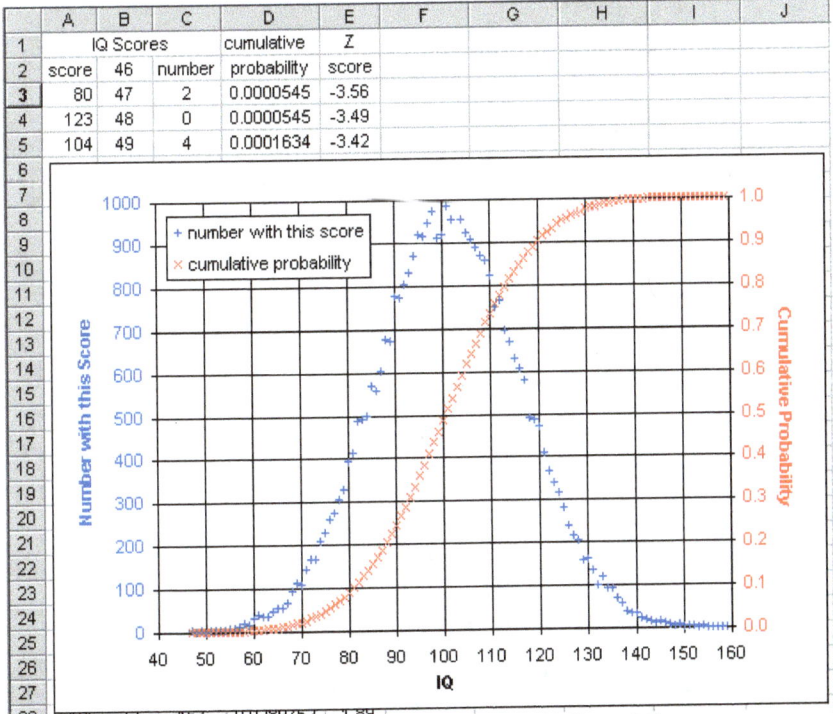

Figure 45. Typical IQ Scores Forming Bell-Shaped Curve

The blue +s indicate the number of persons with each score and the red xs indicate the cumulative probability. The blue +s have the familiar bell shape and the red xs are the area under the blue curve normalized to 1. The mean is 100 and the standard deviation is 15 for the traditional IQ curve. This is what the red xs look like plotted on a probability scale:

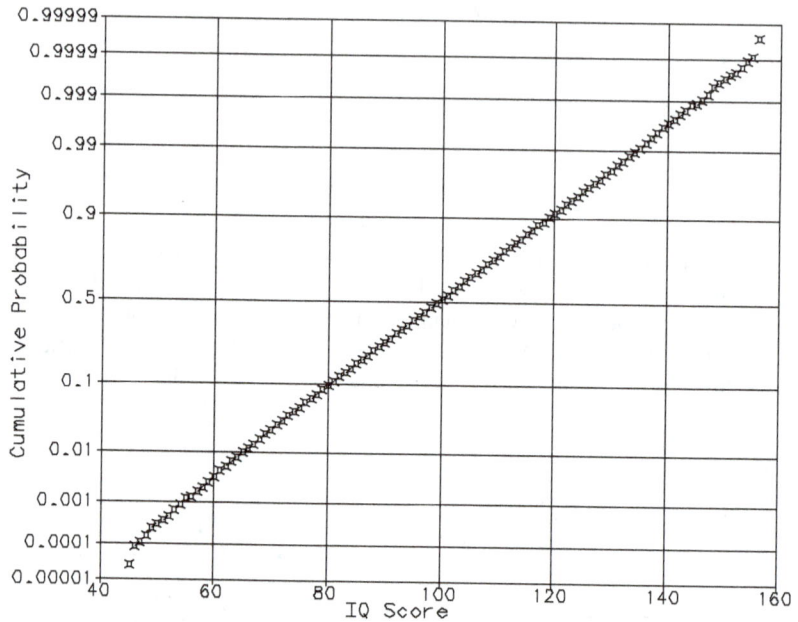

Figure 46. Test Results Re-Plotted as z Scores

Excel won't draw a probability axis. Instead, the z-score can be used:

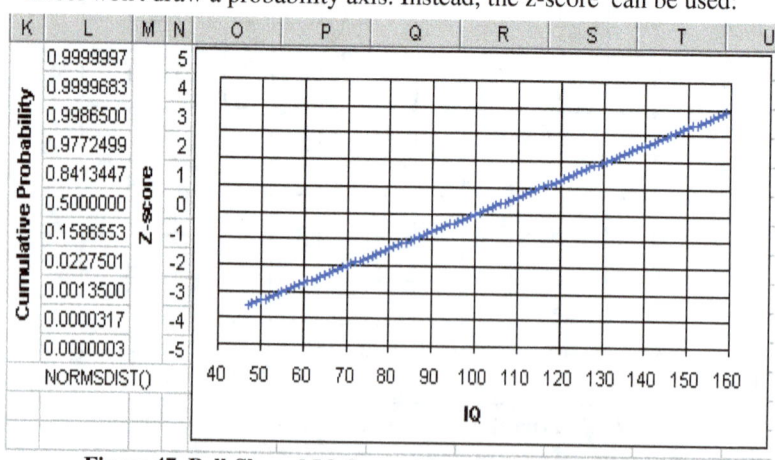

Figure 47. Bell-Shaped IQ Scores Plotted on Transform z Axis

Although the Y-axis numbering doesn't show 0.00001 to 0.99999 as in the preceding graph, the shape is exactly the same. While Excel won't draw a probability axis, it does have functions that facilitate working with probability. These include: NORMDIST(), NORMINV(), NORMSDIST(), NORMSINV(). The integrated help feature describes these functions. See Appendix B for more details. The following table shows the correspondence between probability and z-value as calculated using the NORMSINV() function:

	A	B
1	probability	NORMSINV
2	0.000001	-4.77
3	0.00001	-4.27
4	0.0001	-3.72
5	0.001	-3.09
6	0.01	-2.33
7	0.1	-1.28
8	0.5	0.00
9	0.9	1.28
10	0.99	2.33
11	0.999	3.09
12	0.9999	3.72
13	0.99999	4.27
14	0.999999	4.77

Figure 48. Excel Function for Transform Variable

Comparing this table with the left side in the preceding figure shows that convenient values of the z-value don't correspond to convenient values of probability. We can use this curve and the functions provided by Excel to see how many people might we expect to have an IQ of 110, 120, 130, etc. or 90, 80, 70, etc. In order to calculate this we begin with a score (e.g., 110), using the mean (100) and standard deviation (15), we calculate z=+0.67. We use Excel's NORMDIST function to arrive at a probability of p=0.748. The frequency of occurrence would then be 1/(1-p)=3.96 or we would expect about one out of 4 people to have an IQ of 110 or above. As the bell-shaped curve is symmetric (which may or may not realistically be true for human IQ), we would also expect one out of 4 people to have an IQ of 90 or below.

We can also work backwards to find out what IQ corresponds to one in 1000. The probability is p=1/(1-1000)=0.999. We get the corresponding z by calling NORMSINV(0.999)=3.09 and use this to get IQ=100+3.09×15=146.35 so that we expect one in a thousand people will have an IQ of 146 or above and 54 or below. What about one in a million? p=1/(1-1,000,000)=0.999999; z=4.77; IQ=171.53 or –4.77 to get 28.69; so a person having an IQ of 172 or above (and 29 or below) would be one in a million. The following table lists a range of values. Of course, the mean IQ (100) corresponds to a frequency of 2 (half above and half below).

Table 19.1 IQ Scores, Probability, and Frequency

IQ	Z	probability	frequency
200	6.67	0.99999999999	76,017,176,740
190	6.00	0.999999999	1,009,976,678
180	5.33	0.99999995	20,696,863
171.53	4.77	0.9999990	1,000,000
170	4.67	0.999998	652,598
160	4.00	0.99997	31,560
150	3.33	0.9996	2,330
146.35	3.09	0.999	1,000
140	2.67	0.996	261
130	2.00	0.977	44
120	1.33	0.909	11
110	0.67	0.748	4
100	0.00	0.5	2
90	-0.67	0.252	4
80	-1.33	0.0912	11
70	-2.00	0.0228	44
60	-2.67	0.00383	261
53.65	-3.09	0.00100	1,000
50	-3.33	0.000429	2,330
40	-4.00	0.0000317	31,560
30	-4.67	0.00000153	652,598
28.69	-4.75	0.0000010000	1,000,000
20	-5.33	0.0000000483	20,696,863
10	-6.00	0.000000000990	1,009,976,678
0	-6.67	0.0000000000132	76,017,176,740

Predicting the 100-Year Storm

If we find a storm pattern (for example: maximum wind speed or duration or highest storm surge) that exhibits a normally-distributed probability, we can use these same Excel functions to calculate what we might expect in the future. If, for instance, we have data for 50 years, we might estimate the 100-year or even the 500-year storm. For this example we will consider measured wind speed in Chicago, "Windy City". The data were obtained from NOAA's GSOD, stored on the NCDC. The data can be found in spreadsheet wind.xls.

This table shows wind sorted by date and also date sorted by wind. The frequency of occurrence is accumulated in column E and the z is calculated from the frequency of occurrence using the NORMSINV() function.

	A	B	C	D	E	F
1	measured wind speed					
2	date	knots	date	knots	occurrence	z
3	10/9/1946	9.3	10/20/1954	0.5	0.000038	-3.96
4	10/10/1946	12.1	8/24/1969	0.6	0.000076	-3.79
5	10/11/1946	20.9	7/26/1954	0.8	0.000113	-3.69
6	10/12/1946	14.1	10/11/1951	0.9	0.000151	-3.61
7	10/13/1946	8.5	8/28/1954	1.0	0.000189	-3.55
8	10/14/1946	14.1	7/23/1954	1.1	0.000227	-3.51
9	10/15/1946	14.1	10/21/1954	1.2	0.000265	-3.47
10	10/16/1946	12.7	8/15/1954	1.3	0.000303	-3.43
11	10/17/1946	9.8	1/4/1958	1.3	0.000340	-3.40
12	10/18/1946	16.6	9/26/1968	1.4	0.000378	-3.37
13	10/19/1946	8.2	11/4/1968	1.4	0.000416	-3.34
14	10/20/1946	6.2	3/8/2010	1.4	0.000454	-3.32

Figure 49. Wind in Chicago

This is actual data from O'Hare Airport over a period of more than 75 years. This is the average wind speed in knots for the day, not peak wind gust:

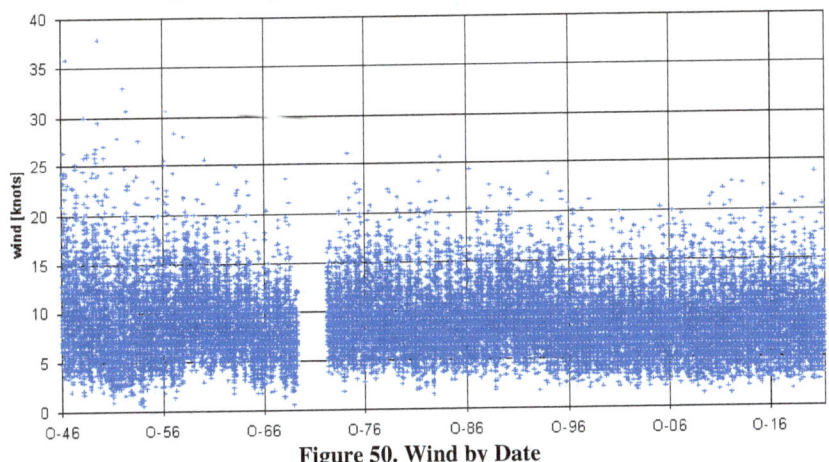

Figure 50. Wind by Date

The frequency of occurrence is equal to $1/(1+n)$, $1/(1+n)+1/(1+n)$, ..., where n is the number of data points. This series begins at a tiny increment and reaches 1 minus that same increment, which is an approximation based on the information we have available.

This next figure shows the same wind speeds, only plotted vs. the z value:

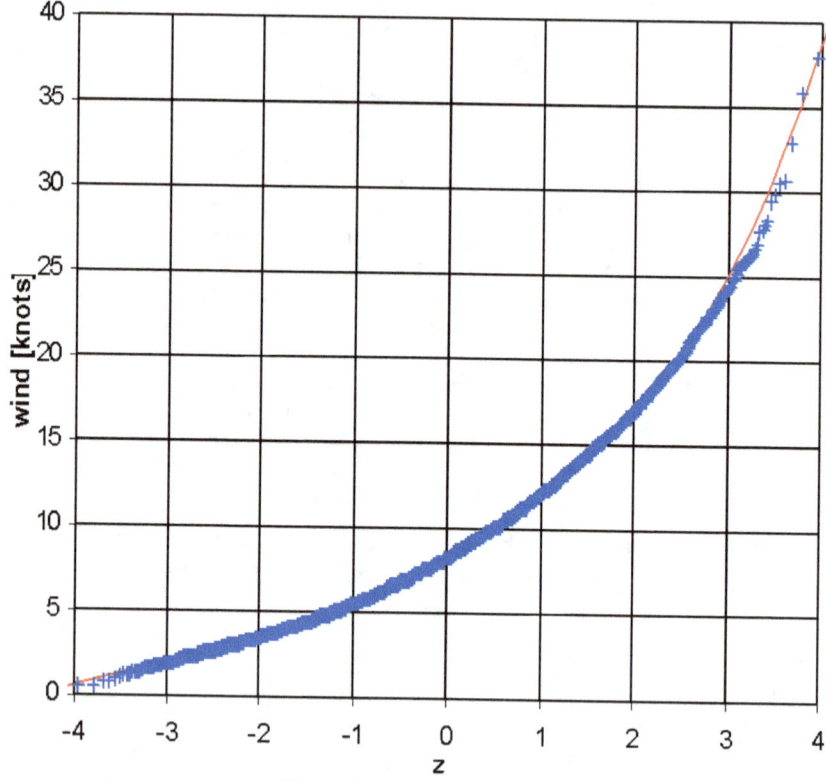

Figure 51. Wind Speed vs. z

We fit the data to arrive at the red curve, which is:

z=(0.525557393654*v-4.37447912578)/(0.0776022204511*v+1)

We can then use this regression to determine the z and then p (probability) of any wind speed, from which we get the occurrence. As this data is daily and we want yearly predictions, we must divide by 365.25. The formula for p is:

p=NORMDIST(z)

and the formula for occurrence is:

=IF(p<0.5,1/p,1/(1-p))/365.25

This is exactly what we would do to predict the 100-year storm or flood event. We have used Excel's functions and graphing capability, which is quite convenient. Before Excel, there was a special type of graph paper, which had a probability scale like that in Figure 46. You manually plotted the data on that paper and drew a smooth curve through it, then performed the same calculations only by hand.

The following table shows several values of wind speed, z, probability, and occurrence:

Table 19.2 Chicago Wind Speed Regression

knots	z	probability	occurrence
0	-4.37	0.0000061	449
5	-1.26	0.1041212	0
10	0.50	0.6900901	0
15	1.62	0.9475399	0
20	2.40	0.9919051	0
25	2.98	0.9985636	2
30	3.42	0.9996904	9
35	3.77	0.9999193	34
40	4.06	0.9999751	110
45	4.29	0.9999911	308
50	4.49	0.9999964	762
55	4.66	0.9999984	1701
60	4.80	0.9999992	3476

We see that a 40-knot wind daily average can be expected once in 110 years and a 45-knot wind can be expected once in 308 years. If we want exact year values (e.g., 100, 200, 300, 400, 500, ...) we can use Excel's Solver to adjust the v to make the occurrence match any desired value. We also see that the people of Chicago must wait about 449 years to experience a day with negligible wind, so I guess it is the Windy City after all. The zeroes in Table 19.2 mean that this happens all the time.

Appendix A. Sample Excel™ Add-In

Excel™ can handle many simple tasks encoded in VBA (Visual Basic for Applications). Many tasks, for example, creating a cubic spline, are not practical in VBA. These and other more complex tasks can often be accomplished within Excel through an Add-In written in C or Pascal. An Excel Add-In has the file extension .XLL, which is simply a renamed .DLL with a specific wrapper, facilitating access to the contents.

The most extensive (and helpful) text on Excel® Add-Ins is that of Steve Dalton.[9] This excellent document can be found in PDF form at several locations on the Web. Add-Ins (and, for that matter software) development is beyond the scope of this text. The reader is directed to Dalton's text for the former and Kernighan and Ritchie for the latter. The Web is replete with information on software development.

Microsoft™ originally expected all Excel Add-Ins to be written in Pascal. All of the calling conventions are Pascal. All of the strings must be Pascal; that is, the first character is the length of the string. This is in contrast to C strings, where the last character is a terminating zero.

The bitness (i.e., either 32-bit or 64-bit) of the Add-In *must* match the bitness of MS Office®. Note that this may not be the same as the bitness of the O/S (i.e., a 32-bit version of Windows® can only run a 32-bit version of MSO; whereas, a 64-bit version of Windows® can run either a 32-bit or a 64-bit version of MSO). In order to create an Excel Add-In you must have a compiler that can generate objects (i.e., compiled code, .OBJ modules) in the required bitness. Visual Studio™ comes in both 32-bit and 64-bit and works well for this purpose.

In order to produce a working Excel Add-In, you must create the code in accordance with Microsoft's guidelines, compile it with a compatible compiler, and link it with a compatible linker, then rename it. Note that Excel, being a Microsoft product, expects object modules in the COFF[10] format, not the OMF[11] format. Some compilers will only produce the latter. When creating an Excel Add-In, I have found that it's best to stick with Visual Studio, though I do use several other compilers at times; for example, Digital Mars.

You will find a sample Add-In containing several functions in the examples folder (addin.c). Follow the instructions therein to compile and link it. Modify it to include your own functions. Read Dalton's text for more details.

---

[9] Dalton, S., Excel Add-in Development in C/C++: Applications in Finance, John Wiley & Sons, Ltd., Chichester, England, 2005.
[10] Common Object File Format (COFF) object-code format for UNIX and also Microsoft
[11] Object Module Format (OMF) used by some early (e.g., Intel 386) 32-bit compilers

Appendix B. Normal Distribution Functions

The Excel™ help information on the NORMDIST, NORMSDIST, NORMINV, and NORMSINV is limited. Given only the information contained therein, you might be hard-pressed to duplicate some of the algorithms. You may also need these same algorithms outside of Excel; therefore, we will cover them in more detail here. For illustration we use normal.xls and normal.c, which can be found in the examples folder. We use IQ scores and the associated bell-shaped curve for our sample calculations. Recall that $\mu=100$ and $\sigma=15$. The following table is a comparison of the forward group of built-in and replacement functions:

		NORMDIST (FALSE)		NORMDIST (TRUE)		NORMSDIST	
x	z	p	check	p	check	p	check
20	-5.333	0.00000002	0.00000002	0.00000005	0.00000005	0.00000005	0.00000005
30	-4.667	0.00000050	0.00000050	0.00000153	0.00000153	0.00000153	0.00000153
40	-4.000	0.00000892	0.00000892	0.00003169	0.00003169	0.00003169	0.00003169
50	-3.333	0.00010282	0.00010282	0.00042912	0.00042912	0.00042912	0.00042910
60	-2.667	0.00075973	0.00075973	0.00383043	0.00383043	0.00383043	0.00383093
70	-2.000	0.00359940	0.00359940	0.02275006	0.02275006	0.02275006	0.02274569
80	-1.333	0.01093400	0.01093400	0.09121128	0.09121128	0.09121128	0.09120636
90	-0.667	0.02129653	0.02129653	0.25249247	0.25249247	0.25249247	0.25282482
100	0.000	0.02659615	0.02659615	0.50000000	0.50000000	0.50000000	0.50000000
110	0.667	0.02129653	0.02129653	0.74750753	0.74750753	0.74750753	0.74717518
120	1.333	0.01093400	0.01093400	0.90878872	0.90878872	0.90878872	0.90879364
130	2.000	0.00359940	0.00359940	0.97724994	0.97724994	0.97724994	0.97725431
140	2.667	0.00075973	0.00075973	0.99616957	0.99616957	0.99616957	0.99616907
150	3.333	0.00010282	0.00010282	0.99957088	0.99957088	0.99957088	0.99957090
160	4.000	0.00000892	0.00000892	0.99996831	0.99996831	0.99996831	0.99996831
170	4.667	0.00000050	0.00000050	0.99999847	0.99999847	0.99999847	0.99999847
180	5.333	0.00000002	0.00000002	0.99999995	0.99999995	0.99999995	0.99999995

Figure 52. Comparison of Forward Functions

Note that there is excellent agreement. The VBA replacement functions can be found in normal.xls

This next table is a comparison of the backward (inverse) functions:

x	z	NORMINV		NORMSINV	
		z	check	z	check
20	-5.333	???	20.00	???	-5.333
30	-4.667	29.59	30.00	-4.694	-4.667
40	-4.000	40.00	40.00	-4.000	-4.000
50	-3.333	50.00	50.00	-3.333	-3.333
60	-2.667	60.00	60.00	-2.667	-2.667
70	-2.000	70.00	70.02	-2.000	-1.999
80	-1.333	80.00	79.91	-1.333	-1.340
90	-0.667	90.00	90.18	-0.667	-0.654
100	0.000	100.00	100.00	0.000	0.000
110	0.667	110.00	109.82	0.667	0.654
120	1.333	120.00	120.09	1.333	1.340
130	2.000	130.00	129.98	2.000	1.999
140	2.667	140.00	140.00	2.667	2.667
150	3.333	150.00	150.00	3.333	3.333
160	4.000	160.00	160.00	4.000	4.000
170	4.667	170.41	170.00	4.694	4.667
180	5.333	???	180.00	???	5.333

Figure 53. Comparison of Reverse (Inverse) Functions

Notice that the built-in Excel functions are not entirely self-consistent, as indicated by the values in red. Excel won't calculate the entries indicated by ??? and is off in the fourth significant figure for the other two. The equivalent C code can be found in normal.c and is listed below:

```
double erf(double x)
  {
  double q,t,y,z;
  if(fabs(x)<0.0000001)
    return(0.);
  if(x>6.)
    return(1.);
  if(x<-6.)
    return(-1.);
  y=fabs(x);
  t=1./(1.+0.3275911*y);
  q=((((1.061405429*t-1.453152027)*t+1.421413741)*t
    -0.284496736)*t+0.254829592)*t;
  z=1.-q/exp(x*x);
  if(x<0.)
    return(-z);
  return(z);
  }
double normdist(double x,double mu,double sigma,BOOL cumulative)
  {
  double z;
```

```
  z=(x-mu)/sigma;
  if(cumulative)
    return((1.+erf(z/sqrt(2.)))/2.);
  return(exp(-z*z/2.)/sigma/sqrt(2.*M_PI));
  }
double normsdist(double z)
  {
  double x;
x=(((0.00491269829888*z*z+0.226256306341)*z*z+1.31706921
487)*z*z
+0.87779133934)*z/(((0.000456826821739*z*z+0.08607906883
67)*z*z
    +1.02941402653)*z*z+1.);
  if(z<0.)
    return(exp(x)/2.);
  if(z>0.)
    return(1.-exp(-x)/2.);
  return(0.5);
  }
double normsinv(double p)
  {
  double x;
  if(p<0.5)
    x=log(2.*p);
  else if(p>0.5)
    x=-log(2.-2.*p);
  else
    x=0.;
  return(((((((((-3.25827445083E-9*x+1.61986324187E-
15)*x
    +0.000018303435409)*x-6.2769338749E-
12)*x+0.00758688240346)*x
    -1.43922019269E-9)*x+0.306055996906)*x-
1.92368212218E-8)*x
    +1.02666429167)*x/(((((((7.81461220935E-5*x-
2.38842480642E-11)*x
    +0.0181678641217)*x-2.89307816431E-
9)*x+0.468538918156)*x
    -2.18209886841E-8)*x+1)));
  }
double norminv(double p,double mu,double sigma)
  {
  return(mu+normsinv(p)*sigma);
  }
```

Output of the C code comparison is listed in the following table:

x	z	FALSE NORMDIST	TRUE NORMDIST	NORMSDIST	x	z
20	-5.333	0.00000002	0.00000005	0.00000005	20.00	-5.333
30	-4.667	0.00000050	0.00000153	0.00000153	30.00	-4.667
40	-4.000	0.00000892	0.00003169	0.00003169	40.00	-4.000
50	-3.333	0.00010282	0.00042912	0.00042910	50.00	-3.333
60	-2.667	0.00075973	0.00383043	0.00383093	60.00	-2.667
70	-2.000	0.00359940	0.02275006	0.02274569	70.01	-1.999
80	-1.333	0.01093400	0.09121128	0.09120636	79.90	-1.340
90	-0.667	0.02129653	0.25249247	0.25282482	90.20	-0.653
100	0.000	0.02659615	0.50000000	0.50000000	100.00	0.000
110	0.667	0.02129653	0.74750753	0.74717518	109.80	0.653
120	1.333	0.01093400	0.90878872	0.90879364	120.10	1.340
130	2.000	0.00359940	0.97724994	0.97725431	129.99	1.999
140	2.667	0.00075973	0.99616957	0.99616907	140.00	2.667
150	3.333	0.00010282	0.99957088	0.99957090	150.00	3.333
160	4.000	0.00000892	0.99996831	0.99996831	160.00	4.000
170	4.667	0.00000050	0.99999847	0.99999847	170.00	4.667
180	5.333	0.00000002	0.99999995	0.99999995	180.00	5.333

Appendix C. Digitizing Curves

The fastest and most convenient way to digitize curves (and what I have done countless times) is to open the source (which is often a PDF) and use the snapshot tool to copy the curves onto the clipboard. Then launch Digitize, which you can download free at the link below the Preface. This will automatically load an image if there is one on the clipboard; for example, Figure 17. This is what you would see:

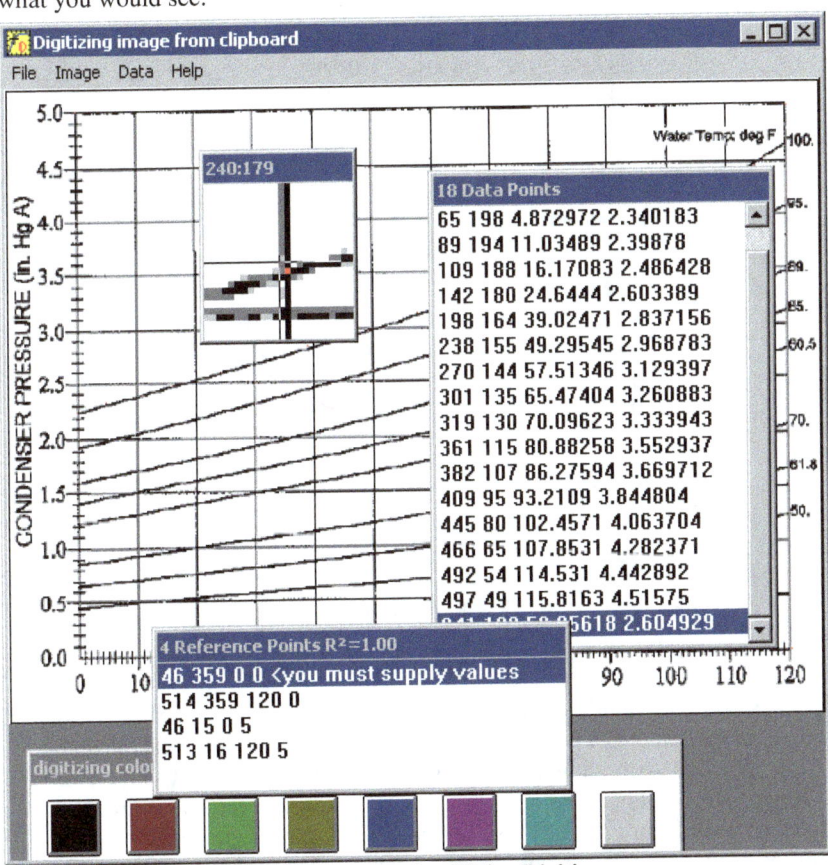

Figure 54. Example of Using Digitize

Next, right click the mouse on each of the 4 corners and enter the X and Y axis values at each point. If it is a log scale, enter the log (for example, -3, not 0.001). Three points is the minimum but I always do four because this enables the calculation of the R^2 for the coordinate transformation. If it's not over 95% then there's something wrong. There is no limit to the number of reference points.

Next left click along each of the lines and you will see points appear in the other window. These will be pixel column, pixel row, X, and Y, based on the transformation defined by the reference points. You can copy the digitized points to the clipboard from the menu. When you exit the program, these are automatically copied to the clipboard. Simply open Excel and press Ctl-V to get:

	A	B	C	D
1	* reference points			
2	46 359 0 0	-0.0641	-0.00363	
3	514 359 12	0.064289	0.003644	
4	46 15 0 5	0.06424	0.003641	
5	513 16 120	-0.06443	-0.00365	
6	* digitized points			
7	46	204	-0.00627	2.252551
8	65	198	4.872972	2.340183
9	89	194	11.03489	2.39878
10	109	188	16.17083	2.486428
11	142	180	24.6444	2.603389
12	198	164	39.02471	2.837156
13	238	155	49.29545	2.968783
14	270	144	57.51346	3.129397
15	301	135	65.47404	3.260883
16	319	130	70.09623	3.333943
17	361	115	80.88258	3.552937
18	382	107	86.27594	3.669712
19	409	95	93.2109	3.844804
20	445	80	102.4571	4.063704
21	466	65	107.8531	4.282371
22	492	54	114.531	4.442892
23	497	49	115.8163	4.51575
24	241	180	50.05618	2.604929

Figure 55. Typical Digitized Points

If the curves were in color and if those colors are in the standard Windows palette of 16 colors and if you select one of the colors from the palette and press Ctl-A, Digitize will automatically select all of those colors. This is a mess if there are colors all over the image and a waste of time if the colors aren't exactly equal to the standard palette. You will need some sort of image editor to manage this. My favorite is Paint Shop Pro™. If you have several curves, each in one of the 14 standard colors (excluding black and white) and press Ctl-Alt-A, Digitize will do them all sequentially.

By default Digitize thins out the selection, as there are often way too many points on a continuous curve. If you don't want the points thinned, you can select that option from the menu. If the image is skewed, there is a menu option to straighten it up that often works well and simplifies the transformation.

Appendix D. Curve-Fitting

If you want a single-variable regression; that is, y(x), or a multi-variable regression, that is f(x,y,z,...), the easiest way of accomplishing this is with CurveFit, which can be downloaded for free at the link below the Preface. Launch CurveFit, copy the data to the clipboard, select y(x) or y(x1,x2,x3...), and press Read Clipboard. You can also read data from a file, which must either be text or comma-separated. CurveFit will not read an XLS file or any other application-specific formatted file.

The data must be in the right column order; that is, x then y for single-variable. The independent variable(s) come first, followed by the dependant one. This is most often done by coping columns of data directly from Excel. Note that formatted data in Excel (i.e., fixed number of digits) will be copied that way onto the clipboard. This means that information contained in additional digits not shown, will not be copied to the clipboard. If you want all of the digits copied, then the cells must not be fixed in length or all of the digits must be visible before copying.

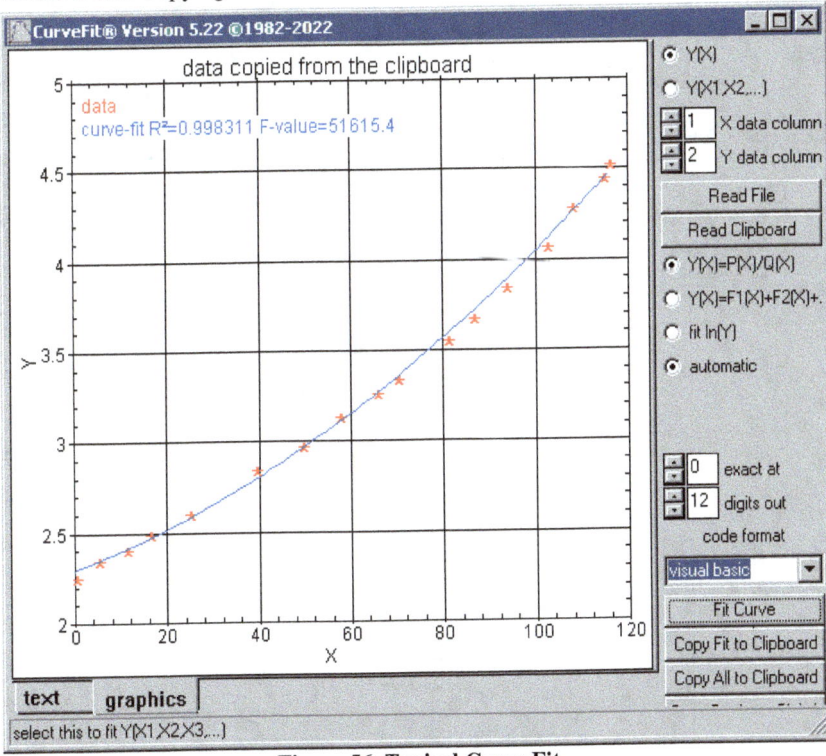

Figure 56. Typical Curve Fit

There are multiple options to explore. CurveFit will create a function containing the curve-fit that will paste right into Excel in the VBA tab (press Alt-F11 to open). Information about the regression is listed on the text tab:

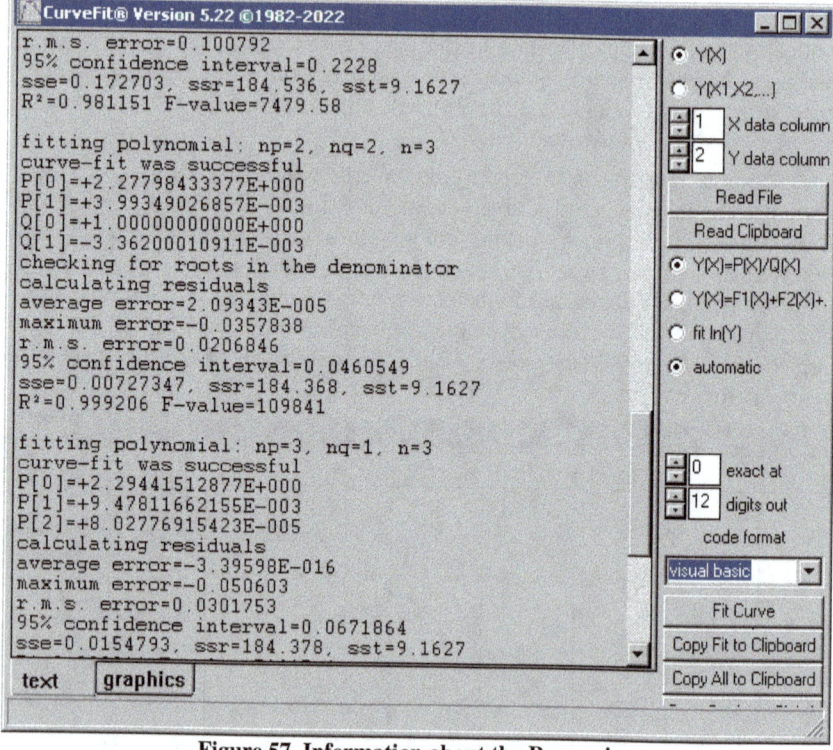

Figure 57. Information about the Regression

Appendix E. Graphing Data

TP2 (second generation TPLOT) is quite versatile and free at the link below the Preface. It can handle 38 types of files, including: 2D, 3D, and 4D. It can also process data, including: converting several file formats and multi-dimensional interpolation. It contains many examples, which are embedded in the EXE file. In fact, you don't need anything but the EXE file to have it all. It doesn't require any special installation and can simply be deleted should you no longer need it.

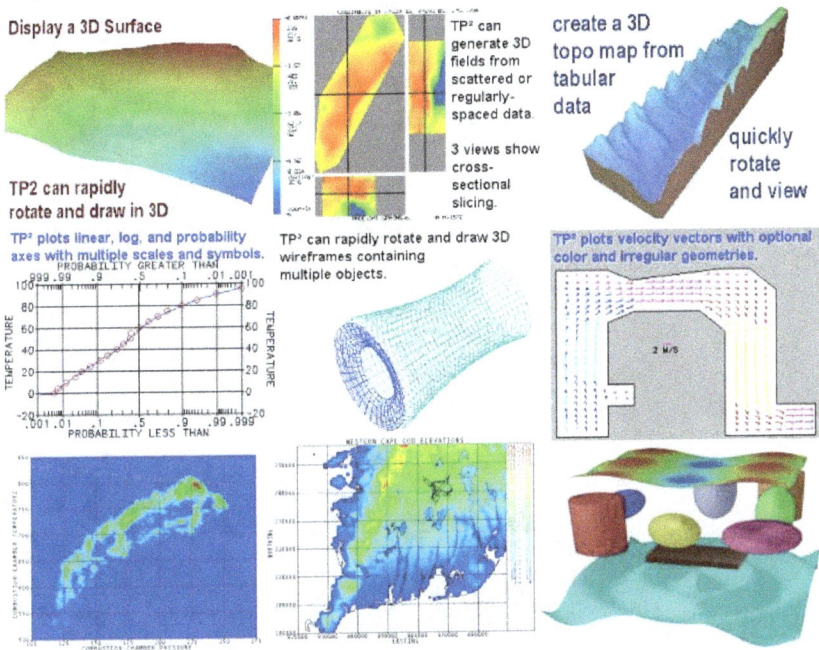

Figure 58. TP2 Samples (all included)

The following file formats are supported:

ext	format
2DS	2D triangular surface
2DV	2D finite element
3DS	3D Studio
3DV	3D finite element
BIN	raw binary image
BMP	bitmap image
CIR	colored circles
CNT	contours (raw)
CON	contours (cooked)
DAT	raw data
DEM	digital elevation
DSM	digital sediment
DXF	drawing
F3D	Field3D
HGL	HPGL
MAP	Field3D
NDE	nodes+elements
NM8	Anim8
P2D	2D polygons
P3D	3D wireframe
PLT	TPLOT
PYR	pyramid
RM	Raster MetaFile
SPH	colored spheres
SUR	surface (cooked)
TB2	surface (raw)
TB3	volume
TOP	surface (topo)
TP2	TP2
TP3	3D function calls
TRA	triad
TRI	triangles
V2D	2D vectors
V3D	3D vectors
VRM	VirtualRealityModeling
WMF	Windows MetaFile
WPG	WordPerfectGraphics
WRL	VirtualRealityMarkup

Menu options include:

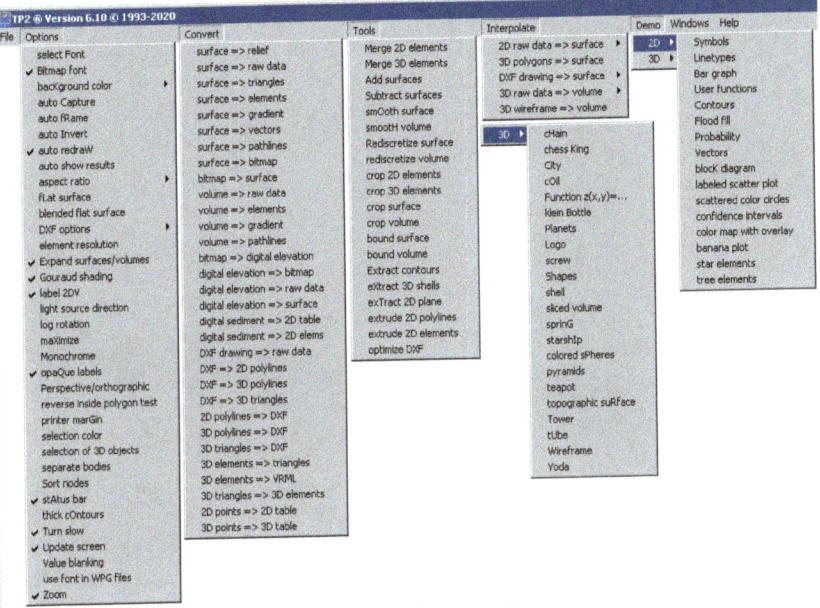

Figure 59. TP2 Options and Features

Appendix F. Editing Polygons

On many occasions I have needed to edit, smooth, straighten, or extend curves. While these operations can be performed mathematically, it is often better to adjust them visually. One common type of curve I have often worked with is topographical contours. These often require splicing, joining, and labeling. There are many programs to accomplish such tasks, one being AutoCAD™; however, it is very expensive and extremely cumbersome, especially for operations such as smoothing or changing the point spacing. As I have had to do this many times, I wrote a program specifically for this: PolyEdit, the polygon editor, which can be downloaded for free at the address beneath the Preface.

Operations like smoothing, growing, shrinking, reversing, joining, and splitting can be accomplished with a single keystroke. Here are some of the shortcuts available with this very useful tool:

PolyEdit Shortcut Keys

Alt-A .... inverts the current selection
Alt-B .... make the selected point the first in selected polygon
Alt-C .... closes all open selected polygons
Alt-D .... deletes the current selection
Alt-E .... changes the point spacing for all selected polygons
Alt-F................... selects the first point in the selected polygon
Alt-G .... "grow" or increase in size
Alt-J .... joins two open selected polygons
Alt-K .... "shrink" or decrease in size
Alt-L .... selects the last point in the selected polygon
Alt-N .... selects the next point in the selected polygon
Alt-O .... opens all closed selected polygons
Alt-P................... selects the previous point in the selected polygon
Alt-Q .... squares the corner of the selected polygon at the selected point
Alt-R .... renames a single selected object
Alt-S................... smooths all selected polygons
Alt-T .... deletes selected polygons shorter than specified length
Alt-V .... reverses selected polygon
Alt-X .... splits selected polygon at selected point
Alt-Z .... optimizes all selected polygons
Alt-backspace..... undo the last change
Ctrl-A .... select all polygons
Ctrl-C .... copies current selection to clipboard
Ctrl-F.................. flip (top/bottom)
Ctrl-J .... joins all overlapping selected polygons
Ctrl-M .... mirror (left/right)
Ctrl-N .... creates a new polygon
Ctrl-O .... opens a new file

Ctrl-Q .... squares the corner of the selected polygon at the selected point
Ctrl-R .... rotate (clockwise 90°)
Ctrl-S .... save and continue
Ctrl-V .... pastes from clipboard
Ctrl-X .... cuts current selection to clipboard
Ctrl-Z .... resets the zoom and pan to full view

Garrett's GTX459R Turbocharger performance curves:

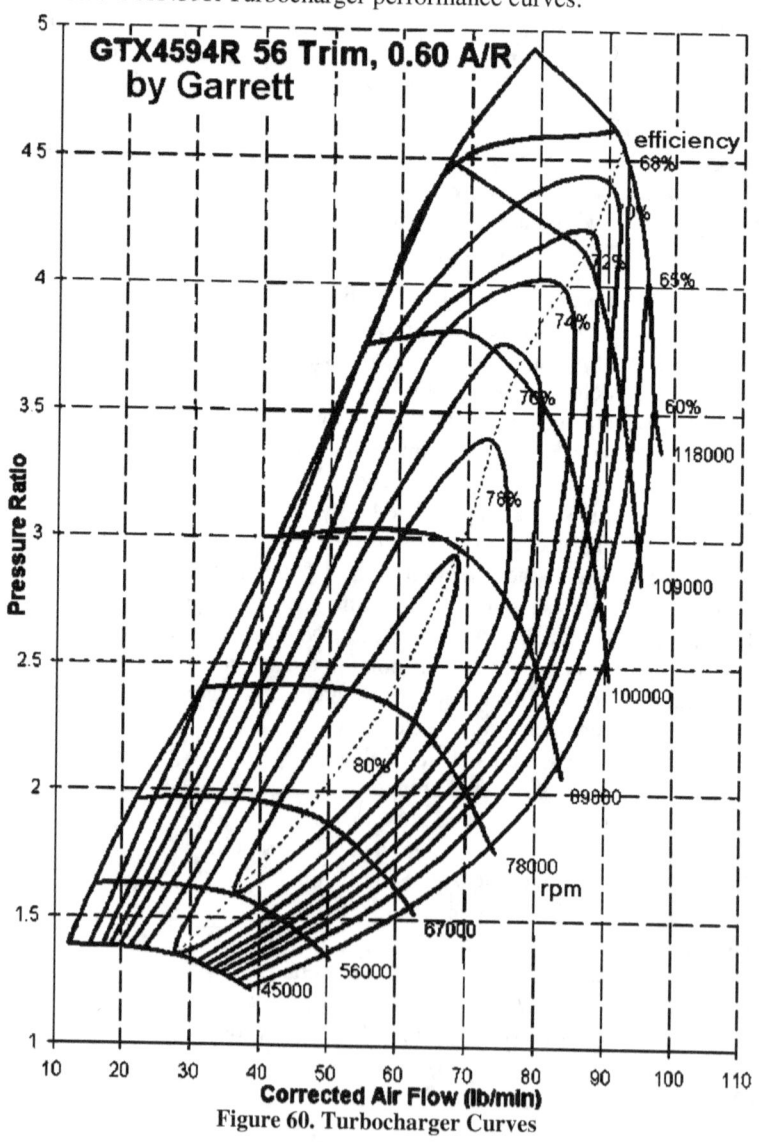

Figure 60. Turbocharger Curves

These can be digitized using the program discussed in Appendix C and then refined using PolyEdit:

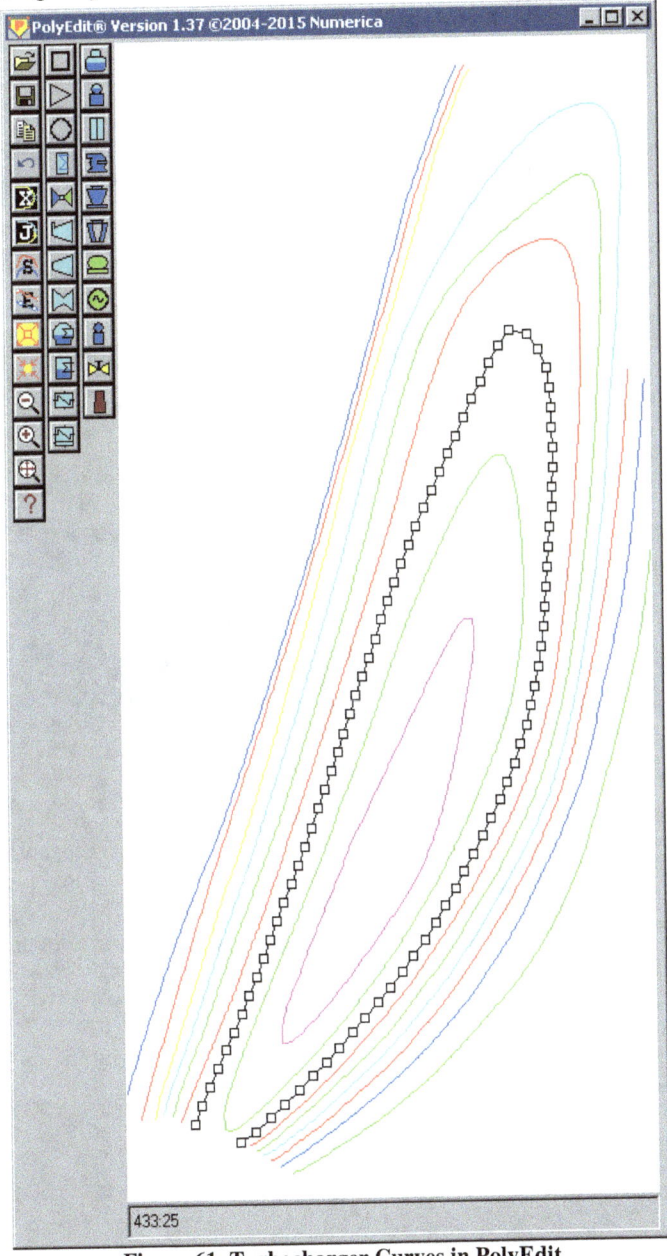

Figure 61. Turbocharger Curves in PolyEdit

The image, curves, regressions and more information can be found in turbo.xls and the polygons in turbo.p2d, which can be displayed using TP2 and edited using PolyEdit. TP2 can also extract and combine contours. A typical field exhibiting a range of values (in this case, concentrations) is shown in this next figure:

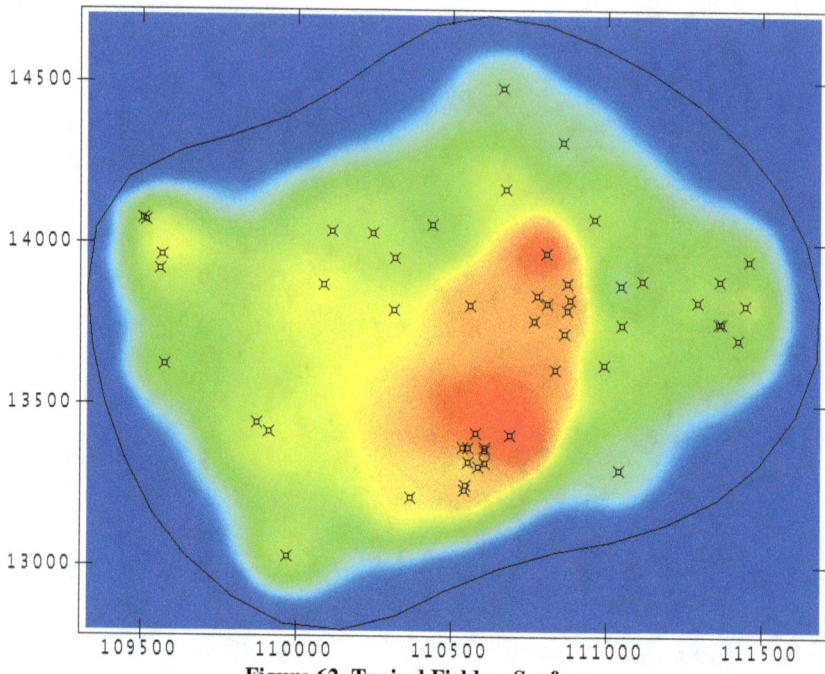

Figure 62. Typical Field or Surface

The contours represent lines of constant value (elevation, in the case of a topographic map or concentrations in the case of a contaminant map or efficiency in the case of the turbocharger performance). Many tools will draw contours given a surface but not all of these will extract the contours and write them out to a separate file so that you can do other things with them, such as refinement and regression.

TP2 will extract the following contours from the preceding map, which can be smoothed and refined using PolyEdit:

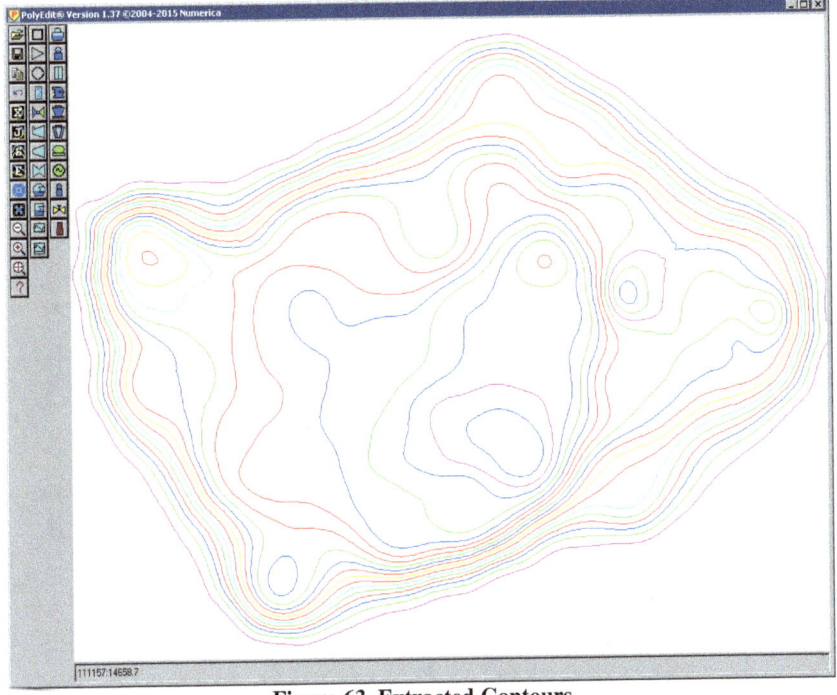

Figure 63. Extracted Contours

As PolyEdit was developed specifically for working with topographic contours, it has an additional feature not often found with similar programs: each polygon may also include a third parameter; that is, x, y, and z, as illustrated below:

```
POLY P1
110032 12862 2
110025 12862 2
110017 12862 2
110009 12863 2
END
POLY P2
109985 12865 4
109978 12866 4
109970 12866 4
109962 12867 4
END
POLY P3
109938 12869 6
109931 12870 6
```

```
109923 12871 6
109915 12873 6
END
POLY P4
109892 12879 8
109885 12882 8
109878 12885 8
109871 12889 8
109865 12894 8
END
```

also by D. James Benton

3D Articulation: Using OpenGL, ISBN-9798596362480, Amazon, 2021 (book 3 in the 3D series).
3D Models in Motion Using OpenGL, ISBN-9798652987701, Amazon, 2020 (book 2 in the 3D series.
3D Rendering in Windows: How to display three-dimensional objects in Windows with and without OpenGL, ISBN-9781520339610, Amazon, 2016 (book 1 in the 3D series).
A Synergy of Short Stories: The whole may be greater than the sum of the parts, ISBN-9781520340319, Amazon, 2016.
Azeotropes: Behavior and Application, ISBN-9798609748997, Amazon, 2020.
bat-Elohim: Book 3 in the Little Star Trilogy, ISBN-9781686148682, Amazon, 2019.
Boilers: Performance and Testing, ISBN: 9798789062517, Amazon 2021.
Combined 3D Rendering Series: 3D Rendering in Windows®, 3D Models in Motion, and 3D Articulation, ISBN-9798484417032, Amazon, 2021.
Complex Variables: Practical Applications, ISBN-9781794250437, Amazon, 2019.
Compression & Encryption: Algorithms & Software, ISBN-9781081008826, Amazon, 2019.
Computational Fluid Dynamics: an Overview of Methods, ISBN-9781672393775, Amazon, 2019.
Computer Simulation of Power Systems: Programming Strategies and Practical Examples, ISBN-9781696218184, Amazon, 2019.
Contaminant Transport: A Numerical Approach, ISBN-9798461733216, Amazon, 2021.
CPUnleashed! Tapping Processor Speed, ISBN-9798421420361, Amazon, 2022.
Curve-Fitting: The Science and Art of Approximation, ISBN-9781520339542, Amazon, 2016.
Death by Tie: It was the best of ties. It was the worst of ties. It's what got him killed., ISBN-9798398745931, Amazon, 2023.
Differential Equations: Numerical Methods for Solving, ISBN-9781983004162, Amazon, 2018.
Equations of State: A Graphical Comparison, ISBN-9798843139520, Amazon, 2022.
Evaporative Cooling: The Science of Beating the Heat, ISBN-9781520913346, Amazon, 2017.
Forecasting: Extrapolation and Projection, ISBN-9798394019494, Amazon 2023.
Heat Engines: Thermodynamics, Cycles, & Performance Curves, ISBN-9798486886836, Amazon, 2021.

Heat Exchangers: Performance Prediction & Evaluation, ISBN-9781973589327, Amazon, 2017.
Heat Recovery Steam Generators: Thermal Design and Testing, ISBN-9781691029365, Amazon, 2019.
Heat Transfer: Heat Exchangers, Heat Recovery Steam Generators, & Cooling Towers, ISBN-9798487417831, Amazon, 2021.
Heat Transfer Examples: Practical Problems Solved, ISBN-9798390610763, Amazon, 2023.
The Kick-Start Murders: Visualize revenge, ISBN-9798759083375, Amazon, 2021.
Jamie2: Innocence is easily lost and cannot be restored, ISBN-9781520339375, Amazon, 2016-18.
Kyle Cooper Mysteries: Kick Start, Monte Carlo, and Waterfront Murders, ISBN-9798829365943, Amazon, 2022.
The Last Seraph: Sequel to Little Star, ISBN-9781726802253, Amazon, 2018.
Little Star: God doesn't do things the way we expect Him to. He's better than that! ISBN-9781520338903, Amazon, 2015-17.
Living Math: Seeing mathematics in every day life (and appreciating it more too), ISBN-9781520336992, Amazon, 2016.
Lost Cause: If only history could be changed..., ISBN-9781521173770, Amazon, 2017.
Mass Transfer: Diffusion & Convection, ISBN-9798702403106, Amazon, 2021.
Mill Town Destiny: The Hand of Providence brought them together to rescue the mill, the town, and each other, ISBN-9781520864679, Amazon, 2017.
Monte Carlo Murders: Who Killed Who and Why, ISBN-9798829341848, Amazon, 2022.
Monte Carlo Simulation: The Art of Random Process Characterization, ISBN-9781980577874, Amazon, 2018.
Nonlinear Equations: Numerical Methods for Solving, ISBN-9781717767318, Amazon, 2018.
Numerical Calculus: Differentiation and Integration, ISBN-9781980680901, Amazon, 2018.
Numerical Methods: Nonlinear Equations, Numerical Calculus, & Differential Equations, ISBN-9798486246845, Amazon, 2021.
Orthogonal Functions: The Many Uses of, ISBN-9781719876162, Amazon, 2018.
Overwhelming Evidence: A Pilgrimage, ISBN-9798515642211, Amazon, 2021.
Particle Tracking: Computational Strategies and Diverse Examples, ISBN-9781692512651, Amazon, 2019.
Plumes: Delineation & Transport, ISBN-9781702292771, Amazon, 2019.
Power Plant Performance Curves: for Testing and Dispatch, ISBN-9798640192698, Amazon, 2020.
Practical Linear Algebra: Principles & Software, ISBN-9798860910584, Amazon, 2023.

Props, Fans, & Pumps: Design & Performance, ISBN-9798645391195, Amazon, 2020.
Remediation: Contaminant Transport, Particle Tracking, & Plumes, ISBN-9798485651190, Amazon, 2021.
ROFL: Rolling on the Floor Laughing, ISBN-9781973300007, Amazon, 2017.
Seminole Rain: You don't choose destiny. It chooses you, ISBN-9798668502196, Amazon, 2020.
Septillionth: 1 in 10^{24}, ISBN-9798410762472, Amazon, 2022.
Software Development: Targeted Applications, ISBN-9798850653989, Amazon, 2023.
Steam 2020: to 150 GPa and 6000 K, ISBN-9798634643830, Amazon, 2020.
Thermochemical Reactions: Numerical Solutions, ISBN-9781073417872, Amazon, 2019.
Thermodynamic and Transport Properties of Fluids, ISBN-9781092120845, Amazon, 2019.
Thermodynamic Cycles: Effective Modeling Strategies for Software Development, ISBN-9781070934372, Amazon, 2019.
Thermodynamics - Theory & Practice: The science of energy and power, ISBN-9781520339795, Amazon, 2016.
Version-Independent Programming: Code Development Guidelines for the Windows® Operating System, ISBN-9781520339146, Amazon, 2016.
The Waterfront Murders: As you sow, so shall you reap, ISBN-9798611314500, Amazon, 2020.
Weather Data: Where To Get It and How To Process It, ISBN-9798868037894, Amazon, 2023.

www.ingramcontent.com/pod-product-compliance
Lightning Source LLC
Chambersburg PA
CBHW070235220526
45465CB00004B/1426